ABOUT NIC

NICK WILLIAMS is a bes
guide who specialises in inspirational leadership. He loves working with individuals in leadership roles to help them flourish and become a source of inspiration to others. His work shows how to combine the entrepreneurial, spiritual, people-management and business aspects of ourselves in our work. As a result, his coaching clients have achieved amazing results: landmark hotels, globally successful TV series, pioneering schools, publishing success and influential businesses.

For twenty-one years, Nick was involved with the Alternatives programme in Piccadilly, London, where he met and hosted many of the leading thinkers in the spheres of creative, personal and spiritual development. His own books include the ground-breaking *The Work We Were Born to Do*. He gives talks at events and conferences around the world, and has been invited by many household-name companies to speak to their employees and leadership teams. His work has been featured widely in the media.

To find out more, visit:

www.iamnickwilliams.com

OTHER BOOKS BY NICK WILLIAMS

The Work We Were Born to Do

Unconditional Success

Powerful Beyond Measure

The 12 Principles of the Work We Were Born to Do

How to Be Inspired

Passions into Profits

The Business You Were Born to Create

The Book You Were Born to Write

Resisting Your Soul

Please Quote Me! Vol. 1: Understanding and Beating Resistance

Pivotal Moments

Please Quote Me! Vol. 2: Being a Powerful and Willing Collaborator with the Mystery of Inspiration

Please Quote Me! Vol. 3: Higher Purpose Leadership – leading from your soul

Please Quote Me! Vol. 4: The Calling You Were Born For – my favourite thoughts on callings, vocations and what you were born to do

Leading with Love: In Conversation with Liz Trubridge

BE INSPIRED.
BE INSPIRING.
BE YOURSELF.

Your power to enable the best
in yourself and others

NICK WILLIAMS

First published in Great Britain in 2019.

Printed and bound in Great Britain by CPI Print.

ISBN: 978-1-9160498-0-2

The author is grateful for permission to quote 'I am not I' by Juan Ramón Jiménez (translated by Robert Bly), and has requested permission to use 'How to Write a Book' by Philip Pullman. Every effort has been made to contact copyright holders, but if any have been inadvertently overlooked, the author will be pleased to make the necessary arrangement at the first opportunity.

Contents

A Blessing

The world needs your leadership and inspiration; there are people hungry for you to show up authentically, allowing yourself to be seen for who you are, fulfilling your potential and expressing your skill. There is a light you bring that is part of your unique presence, expressed through your gifts and talents. Claim it:

May you find your true power to inspire and enable others.

May you have the courage to blossom into being more fully yourself.

May you receive insights, inspiration, and clarity.

May you honour your desire to inspire.

May you love and appreciate your own talents and encourage and celebrate the talents of others.

May you find the courage to be open about your humanity.

May you deeply know that you are powerful and resourceful, and you have what it takes.

May you show up in your grandeur.

May you be delivered to your own brilliance.

May you know your own loving and pioneering nature.

May you encourage others through encouraging yourself.

May you realise your true significance and purpose.

May you find the courage to show up authentically and offer inspiration, for the good of us all.

May you understand your resistance and consistently move beyond it so you continue to grow in confidence.

May you dissolve your need to control.

May you embrace your seeming weaknesses and grow in inner strength.

Introduction

A friend of mine was once parachuted in to lead a project, but found the task difficult because some of the relationship dynamics were quite challenging to handle. The six-month project became a bit of a nightmare, and she felt like she had failed to do the job she knew she was capable of, although she managed to deliver the result that was required of her.

Yet, as the project came to an end, the people in her team threw a party, and gave her a leaving card. It said: 'Thank you for the light you brought.' My friend was shocked, because the message was so counter to the story she had been telling herself.

But it got me thinking that most of us have no idea of the light we bring. Great leaders are stars in that they offer the light we need, rather than seeking the limelight themselves. While we are all capable of bringing light to a situation, we mostly don't realise this, or we might think we're being arrogant if we suspect we do. Without knowing it, my friend had brought a guiding presence to the team, as well as the skills and experience needed to enable them to deliver the project. She brought her power with people. As she shared her light with them, she caused others to awaken and remember to their own light.

I have always been fascinated by the power we have *with* each other, because traditionally power is defined as a force we exert *over* each other. To me, great leadership is about the power we have with each other, not the desire to control or dominate anyone else.

One of the key reasons I wrote this book is offer you a fundamental distinction that can transform your view of leadership: that *being* a leader in the traditional sense and *offering* leadership are two very different things. If we believe that being a leader is just about wielding power *over* other people, the whole prospect of leadership might seem unappealing: many of us won't want to be leaders or run an organisation, as even the very word 'leader' comes with a lot of baggage and judgement around it.

The good news is that we can choose to offer leadership in any moment, whatever our official place in the hierarchy. We don't need anyone else to anoint, appoint or vote for us to legitimise our leadership. Through my work with some truly inspired and inspiring leaders, I have come to create an alternative definition of leadership. It means that every act of love, inspiration, creativity, beauty or reconciliation can potentially become an act of leadership. Inspired leadership can be the cause of wonderful transformation.

Leadership, then, it is not something we need to compete over, play politics around, or make anyone else lose out for. It is our choice in any moment: you can show up in leadership, and no one can stop you! By showing up, I mean being authentic, expressing your true inner nature, and claiming your power.

But the not-so-good news is that our choice to respond to our calling and show up in order to offer leadership will probably be met with a lot of internal resistance and fear.

In thirty years so far, I have not found a magic wand that we can wave to give ourselves a free pass on resistance. What I have learned, though, is that by devoting ourselves to leadership and creative work in the face of resistance, a miraculous alchemy and transformation occur. You will gradually get past your resistance. You will liberate yourself. Your soul becomes freer, and you become less afraid and more confident. You stop attacking yourself and instead become more of a champion for yourself, as well as for others.

I wrote this book to validate your inner call to offer leadership to the people you care about. The world needs you to show up in your grandeur of spirit.

As you will discover, offering inspiring leadership is not about learning bolt-on techniques: it starts with being more naturally yourself and letting your humanity show. It is about being open and real, and understanding that you touch something universal as you share your personal experience. Then you are more likely to draw out the humanity in other people, including that of your teams and colleagues.

Leadership can be a chore – or it can be a calling. The same job can have a very different purpose. It is all about our intention, which pervades everything we do. When we access inspiration in our leadership, I personally think we are tapping into a divine source.

I want to see and help incubate more inspired and enabling leadership in this world. I want there to be more leaders who seek to draw the best out of themselves and others, who want to be the cause of more people shining and being their best selves, sharing their finest qualities with the world.

I do believe that great leaders – including you – are part of the hope for humanity. It's all very well to pray for miracles, but I think it is even more powerful to pray in the hope that we can play a part in those miracles. The leadership we offer can literally be the answer to someone's prayers. If we all showed up honestly, expressing our True Selves in our dealings with others, we would transform the world and restore it back to love. I sincerely believe that.

So in this book, I have shared the stories of many of the people I have met, coached and had conversations with over the last twenty-five years. All the stories I tell in this book are true. However, in some cases certain details have been changed in order to protect the privacy of those involved. I share key elements of my personal journey and experience too.

You may have come across the idea that great entrepreneurs spend time working *on* their business and themselves, rather than just *in* their business. I think this applies even more to leadership: it is so important to work *on* your leadership as well as being busy *in* your leadership. May this book help you sit, think, take time and be more 'in charge' of yourself and how your show up inspiringly in your world.

Nick Williams, London – April 2019

PART ONE:

Your Power to Collaborate with Inspiration

CHAPTER 1: YOUR POWER TO HEAR INSPIRATION

'The primary job of leadership is to inspire.'
Donna Levermore, global director in retail

We each have an inner call to offer leadership, but it is our choice how to respond to that call. I believe that if we listen to our inspiration, we can begin to understand how powerful we already are.

Individual Expression Creates a Universal Resonance
Kurt had always been inspired by hotels. American by birth, Kurt was originally a financier who had made his home in the UK. He realised he was as interested in the design of the hotels he was financing as he was in their business models. He had a dream that one day he would design, build and own his own hotel. He wanted to create something beautiful.

Then, at the start of the millennium, Kurt had a clear inspired vision. At a time long before it became London's tech hub, Shoreditch was still a rundown part of London. However, Kurt decided to create a luxury budget hotel right there, something wonderful that would raise the vibe of the whole area. After lots of searching, he found a car park that someone was willing to sell to him. With his inspired vision, he got funding, put a team together and, in 2005, he fulfilled his dream: the doors of The Hoxton Hotel, Shoreditch opened to the public.

One of Kurt's great strengths is his ability to be inspired by a project and a possibility, to the extent that his vision will open doors by inspiring other people too. People are hungry to be inspired, and Kurt delivers that inspiration to them. In a world full of bland, branded hotels, Kurt was driven to create something unique and beautiful that looks like it has always belonged in the area, rather than being plonked there by a chain.

Kurt and his team sold his Shoreditch hotel and, with it, the franchise in 2012. Although it had become a great commercial success, he was ready to move on. But his inspired idea remained sound and there are now Hoxton Hotels in Holborn, Paris and Amsterdam, expanding as part of a global brand. Not bad for one man's inspired idea. You could say that the idea obviously wanted to exist in this world, and that Kurt was its design custodian. He said yes to his inspiration – and made it happen.

The ideas that once existed only in Kurt's mind have touched something universal. The Hoxton in Shoreditch was hailed by *GQ* magazine as 'effortless cool', whilst the *Financial Times* said the lobby was 'a destination for entrepreneurs working in the cluster of tech start-ups in the area, as well as for those working in Shoreditch's media and creative businesses', and *Harper's Bazaar* described the lobby as a 'destination in itself'. Tens of thousands of people have enjoyed eating, drinking, working or staying at The Hoxton. Kurt was creative in the sense of the Latin root of the word *creare*, meaning 'to bring in to existence', and infused what he brought into existence with his own unique energy and style.

We never know the impact that our inspired and thoughts will have. Some people have credited The Hoxton with being the building the area needed to start its regeneration into what it is today. One inspired idea contributed to the rebirth of the whole district.

Inspiration invited Kurt, as it does you too, to become a pioneer in life, work, business, relationships and leadership, and to step into new ground, to explore and venture. Inspiration is rocket fuel for a pioneering leadership spirit. It invites us to take action. Kurt made money from the sale of his project, and he now has the satisfaction of seeing his idea become a global brand. What's more, he feels the urge to do it again, but this time from a place of greater wisdom, experience and personal sovereignty. He is no longer the young buck; he is the wise elder. He has gone on to become the chairman of Green Rooms, a bespoke hotel for the arts in Wood Green that is designed to inspire creativity.

Wanted: Willing Human Collaborators!

So what is inspiration and what is the most powerful relationship we can have with this mysterious phenomenon? In my view, inspiration is an invitation for us to keep blossoming as human beings and to realise our true potential by turning our visions into realities. Yet, for inspiration to find us, we must first cultivate our openness to it.

The most powerful relationship we can have with inspiration is to become its willing human collaborators. I like the Platonic notion that maybe all ideas exist somewhere without form, but they need willing human bodies and skills to become manifest in this world. When we are open to it, inspiration will seek us out, wanting to work with us and through us; asking us to surrender ourselves to it and to be led where it wants us to follow. It is there, whispering in your ear right now, nudging you with your next project, or waiting for you at the next stage of your current project, but can you hear it behind the noise of everyday life? Inspiration asks us to understand our true creative power and to express it; in this way, inspiration awakens us to the truth of who we truly are.

We are each of us designed for inspiration, creativity and leadership. As human beings, we are created to receive inspiration effectively and act on it; and we rob ourselves and the world when we don't. When we do follow through on our inspiration, we can help create a more exciting and compelling future, not just stay stuck in criticising the present.

We may probably never know where inspiration really comes from – and we don't need to. After three decades of following my inspiration, it is still a mystery to me, albeit a bankable one. Yet I feel like my relationship with it is stronger than ever. Whoever you are, you too have as much access to inspiration as anyone who has ever walked the planet. Why not take a moment right now to open yourself up to this possibility and connect with it?

Become an Inspired Professional

You may have come across the saying that 'inspiration is for amateurs'. There is also the old adage that success is 1 per cent inspiration and 99 per cent perspiration. I guess this is supposed to mean that only hard graft leads to success, not inspiration.

Well, here's what I believe. Without the impetus of inspiration, hard graft can feel meaningless. At the other extreme, while the initial buzz of inspiration might be enjoyable, it will soon peter out without action to make that vision manifest. Real inspiration is not just about the early excitement, but the joy that comes from bringing an idea into existence and offering it to the world. Besides being the creative spark of an idea, inspiration is an energy that accompanies us through the process of its realisation.

Inspiration leads to successful outcomes for those people who are willing to invest the necessary energy, face their fears, grow, become skilful and keep going, sometimes even through their darkest moments. This means that, while inspiration is available for everyone, we may need to develop a professional mind-set to bring our ideas into the world successfully.

There's a common belief that the amateur acts out of love, whilst the professional acts for the financial rewards and status that might follow. However, I would suggest that as a true professional, you pursue your projects because you love them so much. It is too painful for you not to respond to inspiration by taking creative action. So you always act on what you love first, and then you combine that love with entrepreneurial know-how, in order to figure out how you can get paid for doing what you love and how you might benefit others through it.

The Business Case for Inspiration

I have enjoyed Cirque du Soleil shows for over twenty years now, and seen them perform many times in London, as well as in Toronto and Las Vegas. I admire their artistry and the spectacle; and I wasn't surprised when I read that Cirque employed two women in their Montreal office whose sole job was to 'seek out inspiration that could be incorporated into future Cirque shows'. These employees are paid to go to galleries, art shows, fashion shows, concerts and the like to find inspiration and bring this back to the Cirque family. I imagined that this must be one reason why Cirque du Soleil are such a global phenomenon today.

At the other end of the spectrum, one afternoon in 2004, I received an unexpected call from a man in Switzerland. He explained, 'I'm Head of Learning and Development in the Zürich office of PricewaterhouseCoopers and I wondered whether you'd be interested in coming over to talk to our Swiss auditing team about the importance of inspiration in the workplace.'

It took me a couple of seconds to absorb what I was hearing. I'd never expected to hear the three words 'Swiss', 'auditing' and 'inspiration' in the same sentence. Part of me wondered whether it was April Fool's Day, or whether I was on *Candid Camera*, being filmed to see how I would respond to this unusual request. I composed myself and came up with a question to check whether it was for real.

'That sounds really interesting,' I said. 'Can I ask you what the business case is for wanting me to run a session on inspiration for you?'

He replied, 'The team we want you to talk to are auditors with several years' experience, who are about to become managers and leaders of other, younger auditors. We know that these younger auditors have different values and it's a competitive market. These young people want to work for someone who they find inspiring and they want their work to be meaningful. Otherwise, quite frankly, they're likely to leave. So we want you to talk about why inspiration is so important. Can you help?'

Wow, he really had thought this through. I asked a few more questions, then said, 'Yes!' and a couple of months later, I travelled to Zürich and ran my session. It went very well, so

I was invited back to run a module on their in-house course for three years in row.

I subsequently found out more about the 'left-brain' (rational) justification for the power and importance of inspiration in business. In the UK, *The Sunday Times* published a feature on '100 Best Companies to Work For', which stated: 'Inspiration rather than perspiration is the key ingredient for a successful company with a motivated workforce.' It went on to claim: 'If you find your boss inspirational, the chances are you will be far happier and more productive at work. The energy and inspirational qualities of a company's leaders emerge as the major factors in making a company one of the best to work for.' In a similar vein, a report by The Chartered Institute of Management noted: 'One third of respondents have never worked for or been motivated by, an exceptional leader, and only a third say their present leader creates a feeling of energy in their organisation.'

There is considerable evidence that there is a real need for inspiration in the workplace, which means the real question is: 'How do we become more personally inspired and inspiring so we can lead the way?' This is one of the major reasons why I wrote this book.

Inspiration Can Feel like an Invitation to Defy Gravity

This might seem one of the most challenging times in history in which to find inspiration. These days, I don't often watch the news and think to myself, 'Wow, isn't this the most inspiring time to be alive! There's so much harmony, peace and agreement in the world. We're all coming together as one to solve the problems we face...' In the current climate, we tend to think precisely the opposite.

What I have come to see and understand is that inspiration means *becoming the cause* of our circumstances, not believing that we are simply the victims of its effects. It's about creating from the inside out. Ultimately, you might have to be the one to generate the inspiration you've been seeking. The most important factor with inspiration is not what is going on in the outside world, but what is stirring inside us. In this respect, the world is created out of our thinking, not out of sticks and stones. When more of us think in inspired ways, we really can change the world, as well as be personally transformed. Inspiration is about a larger causality, an inside job; it is one of the driving forces behind our evolution as a species.

There might well be justifiable reasons why we can say, 'I can't be inspired, because…' Yet every inspired individual can defy the gravity of convention, social programming and conditioning, and rise to help others to rise above these too. Metaphorically speaking, inspired ideas and inspired people 'vibrate' at a different frequency to many non-inspired people, bringing vitality and dynamism in their wake.

Inspiration and brutality seem to be two ways in which we try to change the world. Well, I vote for the inspired way forward.

Finding Inspiration in Unexpected Places

I have always loved the idea that sometimes the most difficult situations can bring out the goodness and humanity in us. That has certainly been my experience.

In 2002, I was blessed to meet Sidwell Nxumalo on a trip to Soweto, a township just outside Johannesburg. Sid was a black master builder under apartheid. He was also a leader within his community and he had created a successful conference centre on the site of an ash dump. I left feeling so inspired to have met him; to hear about the triumph of the human spirit even under apartheid.

In 2015, I met Lola, who was part of a project called The Spark Within. The project did 'Hero's Journey' coaching work with young men in prison, helping them transform their lives. The result was one of the lowest re-offending rates of any programme.

In 2016, I was fortunate to meet Alice, who founded the Luminary Bakery in North London, as a vehicle to train, empower and support women who had been abused, trafficked or imprisoned. The Luminary Bakery is a social enterprise designed to offer opportunities for women to build a future for themselves, using baking as a tool to help them find work and achieve entrepreneurship.

Over the years I have learned that inspiration can exist anywhere. The word 'inspiration' comes from the Latin *inspirare* – to breathe or blow into. Where there is breath, there is inspiration; it is part of the air we breathe.

Quit Searching, Start Remembering

Although it's unscientific in that it can't be 'proved', I resonate with the idea that we don't arrive here on Earth as blank slates, but as highly individuated souls, possibly even the veterans of many lifetimes. We are not just a product of social conditioning and what this has imprinted upon us; we are whole and complete souls who arrive here each with a unique calling. We have a destiny to fulfil, a person to become and a purpose – and that purpose or calling is etched upon our hearts. We have all been called to contribute to a higher purpose as well as our earthly existence. If you like, not only does the creative Muse of inspiration serve us, but we all serve the Muse and the greater good.

I like the idea that inspiration is a mechanism that enables us to remember our true purpose in life, acting like a direct line to our soul and our soul memory. When we experience true inspiration, this is our soul saying, 'Bullseye!'

Your soul already knows your calling, and it's ready to fulfil it; it is only the voice of your ego that is trying to hide your calling from you.

Finding Your Inner Source of Inspiration

Searching for inspiration outside ourselves can be fun and sometimes necessary, but it can also be a ploy used by the ego to ensure we never find it. Such a search can take up a lot of time and energy, keeping us distracted for years. The spiritual text *A Course in Miracles* puts it well: 'The ego has a secret mantra – seek but don't find.' Some of us get caught up for years in the external quest for inspiration.

However, finding our own inner source of inspiration is where our creative power truly lies. That's why those moments of recognition and remembering are to be treasured, when something inside us finds what we had been seeking, and invites us to devote ourselves to what we have in some sense 'remembered'.

We can remember what some people might call a 'soul promise'; we experience a sense of recognition and a realisation: 'This is it. I can call off the search.' I experienced this when I gave my first public talk at a conference in 1986. I had this feeling: 'This is what I'm on Earth to do!' Also, when I came across *A Course in Miracles* in 1996, I had the sense: 'This is it; this is your spiritual path for the rest of your life. You can stop searching now. Now, you can keep going deeper.'

Inspiration can be a More Powerful Source of Energy than Motivation Alone

When we are inspired, we are responding to our inner impulses rather than to external stimuli. Inspiration is like finding your mojo again and can act like smelling salts for the soul. It's this that can make inspiration so much more powerful than motivation.

So often, motivation involves trying to force ourselves to do something, or responding to other people's demands or requests, and either being compliant or rebellious in response to these factors. We can feel compelled to act out of fear or guilt; similarly, motivation can take the form of shame or the fear of guilt or shame.

Yet when we are inspired, we are accessing a natural, innate willingness. We don't have to be forced; we want to do it, we'd love to do it. We can be motivated by fear, guilt, by hurt, by revenge and punishment – but we are inspired by love, and in this way, inspiration is both a source of ideas and a source of fuel.

Inspiration Invites Us to Create, One Step at a Time

Some say that motivation is when you get hold of an idea, whereas inspiration is when an idea gets hold of you. I like to imagine that inspiration has an awareness of how things work for us on a human level. Whilst it often gives us a vision, it knows we create that vision one step at a time, one action at a time. And that there is always a small step we *can* take. It walks next to us on our journey, guiding us and cheering us every part of the way.

Consequently, though, inspiration can inadvertently trigger feelings of impatience and frustration. When we get truly inspired, the distance between where we are now and where we want to be can seem so insurmountable that this can threaten to demotivate us. We doubt whether we can bridge the gap. We want to be there, now; not feel we have to go on a journey to get there. We look for short cuts and hacks. We don't want to do the work needed to get there.

As the saying goes, a journey of five thousand miles starts with the first step. Yet we often resist the small, cumulative baby steps because they don't seem sexy enough, or they don't seem to cover enough ground to be worthwhile. But that is the magic of inspiration. Each step we take allows us to access even more of life's magic. Since the boat can't change the direction of the wind, we raise our sails to access the wind that is already there. By identifying the smallest next step you can take, you can get yourself out of a rut and back into your flow.

By taking baby steps, and starting small in the direction of your goal, you will get into your flow and access the spiritual slipstream. In my experience, when we achieve this, we find an abundance of life-changing possibilities. What is rarer are the people who are willing to take the thousands, even millions, of the baby steps required to bring these possibilities to fruition.

Radio Inspiration – Choice, Not Chance

Let's be clear: the availability of inspiration is not the issue. Inspiration is always being broadcast to us. The question is: are we tuned into it? It's important to understand that inspiration is continually available 'out in the world' when we have the eyes to see it. The world is full of creative expression, love, kindness, forgiveness, healing, inspired and caring people, doing amazing things and wanting to make the world better, whether we are aware of them or not.

However, we might not know how to open ourselves up to access the inspiration that is there, or we might have created blocks in our minds that don't allow us to hear inspiration speaking to us. The fact is that inspiration is a choice, not a chance. This might make a great t-shirt slogan, but it's actually true. We can choose to change channels and tune in to it. An inspired and creative life is ours for the choosing.

If we accept the truth of this, we can begin to accept that it being inspired is not a lucky chance, but a conscious choice we can make in each moment. Nevertheless, we might feel like inspiration is a choice that isn't always available to us. Perhaps our circumstances or where we are emotionally seem to preclude us from following our inspiration. Also, most of us have been brought up to believe that inspiration isn't something we rely on. It is capricious, we believe. It comes and goes, and could easily leave us high and dry.

Very few of us have been brought up to believe in the reality that inspiration is not just for the gifted few, but that it is constantly being broadcast 24/7 to each and every one of us. Our capacity to be a receiver of inspiration might be where the hiccup lies. In Chapter 3, I will share with you how you can consciously nurture your connection with the voice of inspiration so that you are consistently tuned in to it.

Your Creative Power Acts in Anticipation of Inspiration
The ground-breaking artist Picasso famously said, 'Inspiration does exist, but it has to find you working.' While the temptation is to think we have to wait for inspiration to strike in order to act, as creative pros we understand the importance of acting in anticipation of feeling inspired.

By getting down and doing your work, at your computer, canvas, page or in the classroom, whatever it is, you trigger and initiate the flow of inspiration, or maybe more precisely, you will begin to experience the inspiration that has always been there, waiting for you. You access the flow. You come to realise that instead of waiting to feel inspired to do your work, sometimes you may well need to start actually doing it, for inspiration to find you.

Inspiration in Chapters of Our Lives

While inspiration itself never runs out, our sense of inspiration for our business, leadership, way of being or project, can run out. We may lose our enthusiasm, or feel we're out of fresh ideas. This is natural and to be expected as an essential part of our personal evolution. In these instances, inspiration is nudging us towards a new and more authentic chapter in our life, to prevent us from trying to squeeze ourselves into an identity that we've outgrown.

My client Priya was in such a position. She had set up her own dance school, and loved the experience. Now, to be honest, she had grown a bit bored! It had all become a little bit humdrum. The adventure of setting up her business was over, and now she was tired of the routine of running it. What had inspired her no longer inspired her.

This is often when we can get tough on ourselves if we're not careful. We might berate ourselves for losing energy, and can easily turn the issue back on ourselves, wondering, 'What's wrong with me?' If we are not mindful, we try to force or will ourselves onwards, pretending nothing is wrong, trying to enthuse ourselves about what we have actually outgrown. We forget to remember that every ending can also herald a new beginning. What we have outgrown means there is something that is a better fit for us which is beckoning us.

So Priya and I discussed the new chapter that lay ahead of her, and how she might become re-inspired. I was shocked at how quick and deep the impact of our conversations was.

Within a few sessions, she had got engaged, planned the wedding, bought her wedding dress, bought a new house and was planning the move with her fiancé. Not only this, but she had re-energised her existing business, and incubated a new business idea which she planned to implement once she moved house. Wow! Her boredom was a signal all right, but of new adventures beckoning her. She was inspired about herself, her fiancé and her life all over again.

So, if inspiration is always there and communicating with us even if we're not able to hear it clearly, how come we aren't all enjoying inspired and creative lives, and leading the way for ourselves and others? The answer is because we all have hidden beliefs that dampen down and even squash our healthy relationship with inspiration. In the next chapter we are going to shed some light on the hidden beliefs that can serve to block your inspiration.

CHAPTER 2: YOUR POWER TO FREE UP INSPIRATION

Each of us is born to live a creative and expansive life, but we all have unconscious 'contracts' that limit and inhibit us.

Carole asked me to coach her. She was coming to the end of a successful leadership career in a household-name company and entering a new chapter of life, often called 'retirement', a time when she wanted to engage with more enjoyable activities.

Carole had grown up in Scotland and was proud of her hard work and achievements. When we talked about 'what next' for her, we drew a bit of a blank at first. Then she lit up when she started telling me about a course she had been on, which was about collaborative story telling. She enthusiastically described how she had learned to take a group of people and get them to work together to create amazing stories out of 'thin air'.

So I asked the obvious question: 'Have you taken this idea forward?' She answered that she had taken a few small steps but she didn't know why she hadn't got any further with it. As we carried on talking, I had a flash of insight. I asked her: 'Do you take what you love and then turn it into hard work?'

She paused, smiled and said, 'Yes, I think I do. I grew up with a strong work ethic in my family and culture, so firstly I feel a little guilty about retiring and not pushing myself so hard, and, secondly, I do think about everything as being potentially hard work, and I don't find that an exciting or attractive prospect at this point in life. I think that's probably why I haven't moved the project forward – I don't want it to be just more hard work. I've had enough of that in my career!'

This pattern of Carole's was something I was familiar with both from myself and from so many clients I've worked with: the belief that if we are suffering in some way, then we are significant and our suffering makes our work more important than if we are 'just' enjoying ourselves. According to this mind-set, if we enjoy something too much, then obviously it isn't really work; it's something much more frivolous and less significant.

This attitude seems pretty universal: by definition, work is something that is hard, with the potential for suffering, struggling and going against our own nature. It's as if deep down we feel innately guilty and therefore as if we deserve to be punished – and hard work is an effective way of punishing ourselves.

Where Do We Think Inspiration Wants to Take Us?

Carole's ambivalence throws up questions for all of us: where do we believe that our inspiration and creativity want to take us? And do we believe that leadership has to involve suffering and sacrifice in order to have value?

In my experience, most of us are less than willing to go where inspiration wants to take us, so I'd like to explore why that is.

Let's start by looking at what happens when each of us hears the inner call of inspiration. In essence, there are two directions we might believe inspiration wants to take us:

1. Deeper into a life of struggle, suffering and hard work, which could lead to further disappointment and unhappiness. Many of us experience what is almost an addiction or compulsion to suffering.
2. Experiencing more of our True Self and the joy, happiness and fulfilment that are already within us, and which want to rise to the surface. Inspiration wants to expand our sense of Self and shrink our suffering selves.

Often we aren't as creative as we could be because deep down we fear it is going to lead to suffering and misery; or maybe we even believe that it *should* lead to misery and suffering.

Ironically, these sorts of inherited subconscious beliefs and patterns only lead towards more suffering instead, and can be triggered whenever we consider following our dreams. If we don't cast light on them, they can easily remain in the driving seat of our lives, with their foot on the brakes, slowing us down or stopping us completely from following where inspiration beckons us to follow.

Confronting the Restricting Beliefs

Conscious growth can be uncomfortable, but it is more painful in the long-term to live with restricting beliefs than to confront them. Personally, I believe the more we can clean up this kind of restrictive thinking, the more we can become a clearer conduit for inspiration to flow through us.

Here are just some of the ways we make ourselves suffer:

- Martyring ourselves to our careers or perceived duties.
- Forcing ourselves to do things we don't want to do, or to do any longer.
- Denying ourselves the things we love and value.
- Ignoring our own needs and wants.
- Making things hard and over-complex.
- Dramatizing and catastrophizing our experiences.
- Being excessively negative about inspiration.
- Doubting ourselves excessively and agonising over our capabilities.
- Getting into fights and power struggles as a distraction from being inspired.
- Feeling hurt and disappointed repeatedly.
- Creating angst and agonising over decisions.
- Working longer than necessary hours.
- Neglecting self-care and burning out, or otherwise incapacitating ourselves.
- Replaying old hurts and berating ourselves for past mistakes.
- Anticipating failure and future disappointments.

Do any of these patterns and beliefs look familiar?

The Archetype of the 'Tortured Artist'

Many of our restricted beliefs around creativity are variations on a theme that goes: 'to follow your inspiration, you must suffer'; or 'if you follow your inspiration, you *will* suffer'. There is even a version that says: 'You must not follow your inspiration, because then you will *make* yourself suffer.'

This is our ego's distortion of the invitation extended by inspiration. Our ego has bought into the concept of the 'Tormented Artist'. We don't have to look far to see evidence of our investment in this archetype. It's everywhere. Unfortunately, the world is full of examples of creative people who become addicts, or who appear to destroy themselves and the people around them by following their heart and their calling. While I really don't recommend it, if this route appeals to you, just follow these guidelines:

- Be jealous, compete with your peers and begrudge everyone else their victories.
- Drink to excess, or whatever your preferred method of self-destruction is.
- Deny your own needs and put everyone else first.
- Believe that there is a reward waiting for you in another life to compensate for suffering in this life.
- Sabotage your relationships until you find yourself rejected by everyone around you – and then feel like a victim.
- Lurch from drama to drama in life.
- Believe you are 'cursed' and inherently flawed.
- Tell yourself that your talents and gifts are a burden you have to carry for the good of others.
- Overly invest in how others see you and be guided by their opinion of you; then don't do anything that might lose you that approval, including following your Muse.
- Die young and blame creativity for killing you.
- Alienate people around you and then feel hurt that they don't seem to understand you.
- Blame the Muse for killing you.

- Chase an idyll of success and then feel bitterly disappointed when you get there and still don't feel happy.
- Suffer in order to try to atone for the guilt that you feel deep down.
- Guilt-trip others by telling them they haven't suffered enough for their art – or at least not as much as you have…

Obviously, none of these options exactly leave us open to listening to the voice of inspiration. Even if these strategies can work for a while, in the long-term they are likely debilitate or even kill you. You might create well, but longevity will probably elude you: you will burn out or die young. This kind of approach might seem glamorous for a while, until the glamour fades and the suffering surfaces. Amazing as inspiration is, even inspiration can't work with you when you're dead.

Competitive Suffering

I had the good fortune to attend one of Monty Python's live shows in London's O2 Arena in 2015. Essentially, the programme was a run-through of their greatest hits, and one of the best was the 'Four Yorkshiremen sketch', which epitomises the idea of competitive suffering. It starts out with four men drinking expensive wine and one comments that they used to think they were lucky to have a cup of tea. Then, as the men compete to describe their terrible childhoods, it quickly escalates into the realms of the hilariously absurd. The sketch still makes us laugh, partly because, sadly, this kind of behaviour is all too real!

Unfortunately, though, the consequences of competitive behaviour can be far from funny. For a while, I coached both the MD and the CEO of a digital company. From speaking with them both, I got a strong sense of a company culture built on competitive suffering. Senior managers competed with each other around working long hours and making sacrifices for the business. Yet they didn't seem to get much intrinsic satisfaction from their work anymore. They were looking for an investor or a buyer, and they stood to walk away with a big chunk of cash if they could get the business in good shape and make it an attractive investment, so they seemed to me to be suffering now in order to justify their potential pay-day down the line. But the result was that they were beginning to get burned out and wondering if they wanted to carry on. The even sadder thing was that, within the industry, the company was looked upon with envy for achieving incredible success in a difficult market. Yet the guys running it were not feeling like the successes they were perceived to be, because they were – for some of the time at least – a little hooked on their own suffering.

I coached them both to look at how they could achieve success through inspiration, collaboration and clear thinking, rather than long hours and struggle alone.

From Suffering to a Work Ethic of Creativity and Joy

One core limiting belief is that the purpose of life is to suffer, and the more we suffer, the more we will be rewarded in some way in the future. In the West, many of us are culturally affected by the legacy of the Protestant Work Ethic. This means that we have inherited the belief that work, by virtue of its very nature, must be hard and involve a degree of suffering. We can then justify earning our money largely because we *haven't* enjoyed our work. Our suffering somehow vindicates the rewards we receive.

By investing in suffering, struggle and self-denial, we hope we will gain significance and value, perhaps in God's eyes, and line ourselves up for a reward for all the suffering we have endured, maybe in Heaven if not here. So we may even glorify our suffering, mythologise it or idolise it. Suffering is often born out of a sense of broken-heartedness. Yet this ethic of suffering is deeply ingrained in many of us. It can even be an addiction, something we feel powerless to do anything about. In fact, our ego often derives a sense of specialness and significance according to the amount it suffers.

It's time to disinvest our energy from suffering and reinvest in pleasure and joy. Inspiration is an invitation to joy and liberation from suffering.

Self-Acceptance rather than Self-Improvement: the 'Already' Principle

A client, Jack, once said to me: 'I want to write and publish a book, get a talk together and increase my following on social media. Then I would prove that I'm powerful.' The problem for Jack was that he was overlooking the transformative power and impact he had already shown with hundreds of people through his 1:1 coaching, talks and teachings. From his perspective, his power was conditional on him achieving certain things. He couldn't see how powerful he already was.

Too often we are chasing what we already are, but which we have forgotten we are. You may have heard the story of the musk deer, who spends so much energy chasing after the source of the beautiful scent it detects that it never realises it is the source of the fragrance it seeks.

This is a common pattern: we see ourselves as lacking and therefore needing something outside us, so we end up focusing on the wrong things. Our ego tells us: 'You are lacking or inadequate, but do *x* and you will feel OK.'

Another client told me: 'I felt unhappy, so I decided if I was successful, then I would feel happy.' Here he was, incredibly successful in the world's eyes, but still feeling quite miserable. With that kind of attitude, we try to accumulate power rather than demonstrate our actual power: in truth, we already possess the raw materials we need to follow our inspiration towards the fulfilment of our goals and dreams.

Seven Unhelpful Responses to Inspiration

As we have seen, our ego can so easily distort, pervert and filter inspiration, add its own meanings and agendas, or even seemingly stopping inspiration in its tracks. It's easy to 'interpret' inspiration through the distorting lenses of our limiting beliefs.

A lot of the coaching work I do is to help people get out of the cul-de-sac of suffering they have ended up in with their creative projects, even though they might not even be aware that this has happened. An important way is to help them identity the seven ways in which our ego typically creates problems to try to block inspiration and refuse its invitations to us.

1. What inspiration?

I meet many people who simply don't believe that inspiration really exists, or at least not for them in any meaningful way. They believe they are on their own and have to figure everything out by themselves. So there is no point in nurturing a relationship with something that probably doesn't even exist anyway. Or, if they believe that inspiration does exist, they might argue that it has very little relevance to leadership or business, which are run by facts, logic and strategies. I was like this when I was younger; I tended to be very independent and believed that the only thing I could really rely on was myself. I had not had many positive experiences of allowing myself to be dependent on others or anything outside myself. I was a bit of a Lone Ranger, and didn't believe inspiration was something real that I could depend on.

2. We're too busy (and scared) to hear the call

In this response, we keep ourselves busy and distracted when inspiration comes calling, because the truth is that it scares us. We sense it is inviting us to make changes, and that prospect terrifies us. So we dismiss it as a bit of a nuisance, wishing it would just go away and leave us alone. We might greet every new idea with, 'Let me tell you why that will never work!' and carry on complaining about what we have to do to earn a living – all while inspiration is patiently trying to nudge us into a more authentic direction. We dismiss inspiration as being delusional, irrelevant or impractical. If this sounds like you, the trick is develop is to keep the door open to inspiration by remaining curious and open-minded about what it might be offering you.

3. We refuse the invitation because we feel inadequate

We hear the call of inspiration, but we dismiss it out of disbelief in our own capabilities. We question inspiration's judgement and think it should find someone better qualified than us: *Great idea, but for someone else…* Even though we may celebrate the concept of inspiration, we effectively tell it to shove off, at least for the time being, until we feel more ready. We might even share the idea and give away our great ideas: *why don't you do this instead?* In simple terms, we argue the case for our limitations rather than accept the invitation to grow that is contained within inspiration. But inspiration truly does know what you are capable of.

4. We believe it's wrong or sinful to be inspired and happy

If we believe this is a world of suffering and we are here as a punishment, we will probably believe we just need to suck it up and suffer. It's cheating to be happy. In fact, there's something noble about suffering: it means we're here on Earth as a penance and we're ready to pay the price. We tell ourselves we can't, or shouldn't, make a living out of being inspired and creative. But the truth is that we are betraying ourselves as human beings when we tell ourselves that we can't make a living doing what we were actually put on Earth to achieve.

5. We become a slave to inspiration

This can be one of the most common responses our ego has to inspiration, as we saw earlier in the case of Carole. If we believe that life is meant to be hard, and full of hard work that we don't really want to do, we simply believe that inspiration is just going to lead us to more hard work. After a little period of euphoria, we go back to our cynicism and misery. We might force ourselves to follow our inspiration out of a misguided sense of duty, with the result that we end up feeling enslaved to it. We believe we have to sacrifice ourselves to bring our creations into the world, rather than finding joy in the process.

6. We try to control and modify inspiration

We hear the call of inspiration, but as well as exciting us, it triggers our fears, so we turn down the volume a little to make it seem less scary. Then we try to dictate terms to it or control it in some way. We might attempt to set our own conditions – such as allowing ourselves to be inspired but only on our own terms, and when necessary we're prepared to put the brakes on. In this way, we impose our plans on inspiration, rather than listen to its plans for us. We think we know what inspiration really means, without really listening to it properly.

7. We hear inspiration but live a shadow, parallel life

In this response, we gravitate to the area that inspiration is calling us towards, but we play some form of second-fiddle role within it; we hide out. Even if we believe we have replied to inspiration with wholehearted 'yes!' (and other people think so too), actually that yes might be more half-hearted than we think. Within that yes is a hidden set of conditions. We never quite show up as ourselves authentically, instead playing a secondary role to other people who we claim really do have the talent and abilities. We support them, and satisfy ourselves that we are playing a part in the area that inspires us. This is what I call 'living a shadow life' and we will be looking at it more closely in Chapter 5.

All these responses of the ego to inspiration are based on subtle forms of self-judgement, trying to get us to believe we aren't good enough or aren't capable enough to answer its call.

The more aware we become of self-limiting beliefs and the responses with which we automatically greet inspiration, the easier it is to overcome them and accept inspiration's invitation. When we surrender to inspiration and let it take us where it will, we begin to follow our joy and say yes to an expansive life full of adventure, in which we will continually discover more of our latent capabilities, talents and abilities.

How We Face Suffering

Saying yes to inspiration does not, of course, mean an end to suffering. When I was in my twenties, I read M. Scott Peck's book *The Road Less Travelled* for the first time and I was thrown by the opening lines, because they seemed both negative and hopeful at the same time: 'Life is difficult. This is a great truth, one of the greatest truths. It is a great truth because once we see truly see it, we transcend it.' The question is how we relate to suffering.

There is a difference between somehow worshipping suffering and accepting suffering as a fact of life. Likewise, there is a difference between the suffering that can come about as we grow and shed old skins in pursuit of our goals, and the suffering that occurs because of loss or illness and other normal aspects of life. To be human is to have it tough at times and there will be occasions when each of us feels like we are hanging on by a thread. We all deserve compassion and understanding. We all deserve a gold medal just for being human.

So, while we do not need to glorify suffering, we need to acknowledge the truth of what we feel – to allow ourselves to feel all that we are experiencing, in the knowledge that there will be an end to it. Accepting, allowing and transforming our suffering, rather than judging it or wallowing in it, can help heal generational patterns as well as personal ones

Carrying Our Burdens Lightly

In April 2018, I went to the BBC Maida Vale Studios to hear American singer-songwriter Don McLean talk about his seminal album *American Pie*, which was released in 1971 when he was in his twenties. He was now seventy-three and promoting his twenty-first album.

Someone in the audience asked Don, 'Has *American Pie* become a burden to you?'

Don replied, 'Yes, at times, it has been a burden to me.' Then he smiled, and added, 'But it could be a lot worse. We all have our burdens. Mine is writing a bestselling song and album at age twenty-six. I can live with that.'

Don could probably have used his experience of early success to turn himself into a victim of sorts, and maybe he had at times, but at least all these years later he still seemed very grateful for his early success. He certainly wasn't a bitter old man, saying that his whole life was ruined by massive success at a relatively young age, even though people always wanted him to play *that* song; and for many it was the only thing they knew him for.

I think he was saying that we don't have to turn our burdens into extra reasons to suffer. Once you recognise that unconsciously you might have been putting the brakes on your inspiration, you can start to ease off the brakes and put your foot on the throttle. Next, we are going to explore how to say 'Yes!' effectively to inspiration and the adventure of your own life by commissioning and producing your own creative projects.

CHAPTER 3: YOUR POWER TO COMMISSION AND PRODUCE YOURSELF

'Business is the best adventure you can have.'
Shilpa Mehta, Founder of the Paradise School, Goa

Manley had worked in a multi-national for thirty-seven years as one of 37,000 employees, and had recently taken retirement. Yet, eighteen months into his retirement, he felt he was far from done and that he had a whole new chapter incubating within him. So he hired me to coach him to help him explore whether he could start his new business as a coach and personal-development speaker.

Although he had worked in several areas in management, it was clear that Manley was a natural coach: he loved helping people grow and develop. In fact, he was already informally coaching and mentoring six people back at his old company. He wondered whether he could start a business focused on doing this work professionally under his own brand.

So I helped him get to the heart of his work, distil it and then design and develop his first signature coaching programme, including the branding. The next step was to find the first client for the programme and prove the concept, so that Manley would in turn grow in confidence and see that it worked.

One of the easiest opportunities to try out the programme was back at his old company, so he started to put feelers out to people he knew, and within a few days he was pretty much offered a job back at his company. But as we spoke, he realised that he was at an important threshold.

He told me: 'To go back would be the safe option. But that would be my old style of thinking. They would be producing me, rather than me being in charge of myself.'

I reminded him how, when we first spoke, he had told me that he was looking for an adventure that would take him into new territory. For most of us, growth and evolution are the result of venturing into unchartered waters.

So while it was flattering to be asked back as an employee, and it might have proved pretty lucrative, the opportunity simply didn't inspire Manley in the ways he was looking for. In order to feel inspired, he needed to 'produce' himself, to take charge of his work and to have greater self-sovereignty. He needed to change how he saw himself – and also how other people saw him. He didn't want to return to the company as their employee anymore. Again, having been an employee for thirty-seven years meant this didn't come easy to him. It represented a significant aspect of his personal growth.

The truth is that our inspiration doesn't always fit neatly into our work. Our spirit is much bigger than any job we might have.

Self-Sovereignty – the Fundamental Shift

One of the fundamental shifts that I think inspiration invites us to make concerns self-sovereignty, with the power to commission ourselves and to 'produce' our projects, similar to how a TV producer takes responsibility for producing a show. Producing yourself means being accountable to yourself. It doesn't mean becoming unhealthily independent, and it often involves lots of collaborations, but it does invite us to be in charge of ourselves and our output.

Here is how I see it working. Let's work with the idea that inspiration is continually seeking to commission us; it whispers to us and invites us to say yes to the ideas and projects it would love to exist in the world. Unfortunately, as we saw in the previous chapter, we each have various ways of blocking the voice of inspiration. Yet, when we do hear it, we are then invited to commit to doing the work that will cause the project to exist. We are asked to devote ourselves to it, willingly. Nevertheless, we often tend to edit ourselves and effectively say, 'What would you like me to do? What do I have your blessing to do? Is it OK if I do this?' We find it hard to give ourselves the blessing and permission we are looking for to go ahead. If someone else invites us or approves of us, that's OK, but this can make it is harder for us to say, 'I take charge. I take full responsibility and choose to do this – and to make it exist!'

Inspiration Invites You to Become Your Own Producer

'An architect imagines "what if". A builder figures out "how to". Great structures emerge only when the two work well together.'
Simon Sinek, author of *Start with Why*

Some people might regard inspiration as being whimsical and capricious, but, as we learned in Chapter 1 through Kurt's experience, within inspiration lies a very real invitation to take action – to 'self-produce'.

I learned a life-changing lesson about this back in 2001, when I was in the process of completing the second part of a two-book contract with Bantam, a division of Transworld Publishing. I was actually feeling very proud of myself, and, to be honest, slightly surprised, because I was hitting all my writing deadlines.

At the same time, though, something kept niggling at me. I had started recording most of the live talks I gave with a mini-disk recorder, intending to turn them into CDs as I wanted to reach more people and create another income stream. However, although I'd recorded the talks, so far not one of them had become a CD. This was bugging me, and I started asking myself why. What was the difference? How come I had no problem delivering the books on time, but not the CDs?

Then it dawned on me. I was hitting my book deadlines because I was being commissioned by somebody else to write them: Bantam wanted me to deliver the texts on schedule and I was under contract to do so. But nobody was asking me to create a series of CDs; no one was commissioning me. I hadn't made a contract with myself – I wasn't commissioning myself to create CDs!

So what did I do next? Well, I sat down and I had a meeting with myself, during which I turned my vague idea into a definite project, complete with ideas about what I needed to do to produce the first CD. I appointed a part of myself 'Commissioning Director' and then commissioned the rest of me to create the CD. I got sound-editing software and I found someone who could turn my audio files into physical CDs. I then found somebody else to create a gorgeous image to go on the CD label. Finally, I appointed another part of me 'Shipping Director' to ensure that I actually launched the CDs, let people know they existed and marketed them.

I started with one CD, but over the next twenty-four months, I created a series of thirteen, and sold thousands of them all over the world. It was a great income stream; I served more people in more places and I had the pleasure of people telling me that it was great to be able to listen to my talks in the car, on an MP3 player, on the computer, while dropping off to sleep...

Boldly Commission Yourself

In that moment of awareness, a part of my inner character began to come to the fore: this was the enterprising individual who took the initiative, who boldly commissioned himself and who felt inspired to show up in his work, whether he was being asked to do so or not by anybody else. By taking action in this way, I felt I was breaking through the limits imposed on me by an old story that I'd kept telling myself, with the theme 'but who am I to...?' As a consequence, I simply increased the amount of permission I was giving myself and started to champion myself more powerfully than I had.

Many of us are brought up to have an employee mind-set, in the belief that we need someone else to commission or publish us, to lead us, advocate for us or promote us. We believe that only somebody else's interest makes us worth commissioning, giving us legitimacy and permission. Without this, we might sit around waiting to be discovered. We don't see how much power and authority we already have, that we can authorise ourselves whenever we choose to. Often, other people don't even know how much they would enjoy what we have to offer until we show up and offer actually it to them. We create a market as we show up in our work.

Creating Magic through Collaboration

Producing ourselves doesn't mean doing it all by ourselves. We might not have all the skills or equipment necessary to achieve the results we want.

In 2010, I conceived, produced and hosted a course in London called *The Message You Were Born to Share.* In one of the final modules, I invited my friend and colleague Ed Peppitt to meet the participants. Ed had produced several books for me, including an audio book of *The Business You Were Born to Create.*

Ed's brief was simple that day: to help the participants create a five-minute interview in which to get their message across. They would be given a professional recording of the interview afterwards to use on their websites and to showcase themselves and their approach in other ways. Needless to say, the participants loved it. It was beautiful to see their reactions to the results, as opposed to thinking vaguely about doing something like this one day in the future. It showed them how it makes sense to collaborate with other professionals when we need to bring out the best in ourselves.

Traditional thinking often leads us to believe that 'doing our own thing' means going it alone and not asking for help. Actually, I believe that doing our own thing invites us to become a fabulous collaborator, whilst retaining our power and sovereignty. As we have seen, producing yourself doesn't mean you have to do absolutely everything yourself. It might well involve hiring lots of other people to do things for you; however, it does mean you stay in charge as Project Manager.

Liz Trubridge, who you will learn more about in Chapter 8, helped me understand the ways in which production can be a collaborative activity. She is the Executive Producer of *Downton Abbey*, and it wasn't until I visited her office in Ealing, West London and saw the production schedule for series 4 on the wall, that I realised just how much collaboration was involved in her work. The whole schedule consisted of 1,000 scenes over six months, a cast and crew of around 130 people, plus dozens of locations, transportation requirements, and special advisers brought in for specific scenes such as motor racing or dance, hundreds of costumes and props, and then all the post-production work to bring together. All for six hour-long episodes and a Christmas special!

Pioneering Your Own Ideas

Depending on your life experiences and upbringing, you might have been deeply conditioned to seek permission from others, to do as you are told by those in authority, and not to do anything that you haven't been asked to do. It can take a great deal of courage and self-sovereignty to choose to bring your own work into a world that isn't yet asking for it, and which doesn't yet even know whether it needs or wants it.

One of the major benefits of becoming the producer of your own projects is that you begin to realise you don't need a certificate or credentials to inspire and change the world, and you certainly don't need permission to speak up. You don't need to be commissioned by anyone else to develop an idea, or to write a post, create an audio recording or make a video. Change is possible, because it's right in front of you, awaiting your decisions. The hardest part is, in my experience, realising you're in control of the changes you seek to make.

Yet it can nevertheless be challenging to act like a pioneer in a world where many people want to keep things as they are. I once came across a description of the artist, scientist and all-round visionary Leonardo da Vinci which described him as being 'like a man who woke before dawn whilst everyone else was still asleep'. Pioneering a vision can feel like that; we might find it hard to understand why other people can't see what we see so clearly. Sometimes we might even feel like the good we bring isn't wanted.

Becoming the Custodians of Ideas in Time

Inspiration wants us to act like portals in time; to cause something to exist in this world that doesn't currently exist and to safeguard it for those who follow after us. In some respects, we are serving a greater mystery when we are inspired to bring something into the world. We are invited to enjoy a process of creation that could potentially touch the lives of others, across geography and even across the years.

How many times have you personally been moved, inspired and touched by, or grateful for, a book, a song or a film created by someone you don't know and probably will never meet? Pretty regularly, I would imagine. Our ideas and creations have the potential to become bigger than we are; in a sense, we act as their stewards.

I learned a significant lesson about custodianship from my friend Richard, who owns a 1928 Bentley convertible. Although he is this classic car's legal owner, he also sees himself as its current custodian, looking after it for a while on everyone's behalf. Several owners have looked after the car before him, and others will love it after him.

I had a ride in it once, with the roof down, and I amazed at the amount of goodwill the car generated. Other drivers tooted and shouted at us to show us their appreciation of the car's beauty. We got in to conversations every time we stopped at traffic lights. Richard's custodianship of the car certainly brings many people pleasure.

Similarly, when we are inspired to bring a project into the world, we act as its custodian. In a sense, our job is to say yes to serving a greater mystery; we can never know the impact that our project will have until we put it out into the world. I am still amazed that some twenty years after writing *The Work We Were Born To Do*, I continue to receive e-mails from people saying they've just read it and the book has inspired them in some way. There are probably many hundreds more who have been inspired by it that I'll never hear about.

We might never know the full impact of our actions on other human beings. We can simply intend to do our bit, and then to a large degree, let go of any attachment to the outcome. The Hindu spiritual text the Bhagavad Gita teaches:

You have the right to work, but for the work's sake only. You have no right to the fruits of work. Desire for the fruits of work must never be your motive in working. Never give way to laziness, either.

Perform every action with you heart fixed on the Supreme Lord. Renounce attachment to the fruits. Be even-tempered in success and failure: for it is this evenness of temper which is meant by yoga.

Work done with anxiety about results is far inferior to work done without such anxiety, in the calm of self-surrender. Seek refuge in the knowledge of Brahma. They who work selfishly for results are miserable.

I like the idea that as we bring our inspired projects into the world, we are working to serve heaven in some way.

Take a Professional Approach to Inspiration

If you need deadlines to do your best work, then make some up – there's no shame in it. In fact, it's a brilliant idea. Become your own producer, structure your own projects. While you are their custodian, they need you in order to exist; you have ultimate responsibility for their existence in the world, so do whatever it takes to make it happen.

Today, anyone can become their own publisher, broadcaster or producer – but this also means there is quite a lot of rubbish about. As well as inspiration, we need structure and practical how-to information to achieve the best results. Happily, we can simply learn much of this as we go by being professional in the service of inspiration. To cause our inspired ideas to exist in this world, we can use strategies, entrepreneurial insights, know-how and level-headed thinking. To be truly professional is to marry your heart and inspiration with your mind and knowledge.

Think 'Creative Projects' Rather than Goals Alone

When inspiration speaks to us, I think it is inviting us to formulate our thinking in terms of projects rather than goals. Projects are about the expression of creative energy and the process itself, rather than achieving preconceived outcomes.

When I first got involved in the world of personal development, I was introduced to the idea of goals by various speakers. So I decided I needed goals too. I made up a whole load of goals, pages of them in fact. But then I started to notice the sense of emptiness that can accompany even the successful achievement of major goals. Which potentially takes us back to square one, where we either decide to set even bigger and more significant goals, or we are tempted to give up on the idea of goals altogether. Goals can be based on trying to fix the feelings of emptiness, loneliness and lack.

Likewise, goals are often a response to the hopes, expectations or demands of other people. They represent what we *think* we should want. Yet inspiration isn't saying to us, 'You need to feel better about yourself, so here are some goals for you. Achieve these and then you will feel good about yourself.' Instead, I think inspiration is telling us we are already 'It!' – we have always have been amazing, but we have temporarily forgotten this about ourselves.

Psychologist Dr Robert Holden talks about the 'already principle', by which he means that in essence, we are already happy, already at peace, already inspired, already loved and loving. But in our forgetting, we go chasing those things because we think they are somehow 'out there' rather than 'in here'.

Inspired projects can help us to awaken and remember who we really are in essence, while learning, growing and expanding our potential. And when we complete a project, we get to graduate with honours, before moving on to the next project.

Inspiration sees ahead further than we can. It has a curriculum for us.

Is that true? Well, it matches my own experience and many of my clients. Although we often set goals in the hope that we will get to feel good about achieving them, projects can simply be expressions of how resourceful and creative we already are – and always have been.

A Healthy Hunger for Adventure

'Humans are by nature adventurous. The soul thrives on adventure. Deprived of adventure, our optimism fades. Adventure is a nutrient, not a frivolity. When we ignore our need for adventure, we ignore our very nature.'

Julia Cameron

Following your inspiration will lead you into the adventure of your life, although of course there are no guarantees how it will end up. That's the nature of adventure: there is the equal promise of success or failure. And adventure can take many forms. I recently heard HRH Prince Charles describe his life as an adventure when speaking in a programme to mark his seventieth birthday, which seemed pretty amazing from someone who would seem to have everything mapped out for him.

While we might crave a degree of certainty, I believe there is a healthy part of human nature that is hungry to pioneer, to expand, to grow, to move into new territories both within ourselves and the wider world, to satisfy our curiosity. Without this drive, we could easily stagnate and grow bored.

There is an important message in boredom. Boredom is big. We spend billions entertaining and medicating and numbing ourselves in ways to help us avoid experiencing boredom. Yet I believe a major reason we are bored is because we are not creatively engaged – we are not creating. If we all followed our inspiration and became a fraction as creative as we could be, I suspect that sales of drink and drugs would plummet, doctor's surgeries would be emptier and there would be fewer wars and we'd probably live longer.

Become a Source of Inspiration to Yourself
We tend to think of being inspired by other people. It's less usual to think of becoming a source of inspiration to ourselves. Yet you can inspire yourself by taking action on your projects. You may need to find some new companions along the way, and to spend more time with others who are on their own adventure, rather than naysayers who advise you to 'get back in your box'. People who are following their hearts and inspiration tend to be more encouraging and knowledgeable about how you can do this too, rather than why you shouldn't. You have fellow travellers around the world right now, so take the time to seek them out.

Sourcing Your Own Energy – Keeping the Inspirers Inspired

When we seek to be a source of inspiration to others, to be an initiating force, there needs to be a sustainable flow of inspiration for us to draw upon. When we are giving a lot to others, we need to replenish our own wells of inspiration and wellbeing.

I coached Diane when she was taking a break from a three-decade leadership career in retail. She had been very successful in galvanising teams across the globe, supporting and enabling them to deliver some incredible results. She was the energiser and gave a lot of herself in her work, yet when we spoke, she described feeling burnt out and bled dry.

When we started our sessions, I was surprised to hear her say, 'This is the first time I've spent money on investing in myself and my own development!' I was a bit shocked, and it now made more sense that she might be feeling burnt out.

Many of us have grown up with the idea that it is holier to give than to receive, with the result that we can feel selfish if we start caring for ourselves by spending what we judge to be too much time, money or energy on ourselves. With this in mind, I encouraged Diane to explore what would nourish, nurture and inspire her at this point in her life and career. How could she fill up her own wells of inspiration? How could she start to dream again, and feel hopeful about herself and her future?

She was resistant at first, but willing to consider this. She explained that she wanted to continue to be a driving force, and we talked about her own 'self-inclusion,' and how she could give to herself as well as giving to others. Gradually, her sense of inspiration and her pioneering spirit began to return.

The Anatomy of Inspiration

Some time in my late twenties, I came across the writings of Patanjali, author of the *Yogasutras.* Although these words were written over 2,000 years ago, I can't imagine my life without them today:

> *When you work only for yourself, or for your own personal gain, your mind will seldom rise above the limitations of an undeveloped personal life. But when you are inspired by some great purpose, some extraordinary project, all your thoughts break your bonds: your mind transcends limitations, your consciousness expands in every direction, and find yourself in a new, great and wonderful world. Dormant forces, faculties and talents become alive, and you discover yourself to be a greater person by far than you ever dreamed yourself to be.*

From the moment this quote came in to my life, I took it to heart. It was if Patanjali had stretched his hand across the millennia and gifted these thoughts to me. I said to myself: 'Is this really true? Is it just a nice sentiment, or is this a prescription for living?'

These eighty-eight words aroused a deep curiosity in me. I felt what spiritual teacher Louise Hay called 'an inner ding' – the bell rang in me. They helped fuel my desire to leave my corporate career: I wanted to live my life as a conscious experiment and put this quote to the test. What would happen if I truly did follow my inspiration? What would I achieve and who might I become? There was only one way to satisfy my curiosity – try it out.

I do think our inspired ideas often come in a size too big for us initially, which means they can trigger fears and old beliefs, as we saw in Chapter 2. It took several years for me to summon my courage and beat my resistance (see Chapter 4) before I resigned my safe corporate career to start my own business.

Since then, my life for the past three decades or so has been a living experiment – to see what happens when I follow my sense of inspiration, as well as what friends and clients experience when they follow theirs. I have discovered there are at least five significant elements to the anatomy of inspiration, as defined by Pantjali's words:

1. Inspiration is fully activated by our desire to work not simply for personal gain and satisfaction, but to serve a higher purpose.
2. When we are inspired, we access the greater universal wisdom that resides within us. It's like going online, rather than relying only on what is contained on your own hard-drive.
3. Inspiration has its own inherent intelligence and knows where it is taking us: it wants to lead us to a new and wonderful world of experience.
4. When we start to follow our inspiration, our gifts, abilities, talents and forces awaken within us. They were always there, in embryo, but dormant. In the presence of inspiration, we keep awakening and discovering abilities we never thought we were capable of, as if we had been in a slumber.
5. Inspiration wants to take us on a transformational journey whereby we identify less with our limitations and ego consciousness, and step into the power of our soul.

The best way to keep being inspired is to take action on your inspired ideas, to follow through and cause them to exist in this world, in whatever form you work in and whatever your creative canvas is.

The Key Elements of Commissioning and Producing Your Ideas

Below are some ways to become your own producer and turn inspiration into reality.

- Be open to receiving inspiration – and stay true to it.
- Commission your own work.
- Create a structure for your project and become your own project manager.
- Bring your skills to bear and develop them where necessary.
- Collaborate with other people and invite them to bring their skills to your project.
- Keep doing your work.
- Ship your work out in to the world: give version 1 of your project to the world and then develop version 2 of it or the next project – and learn to live with the variety of responses you receive.

As we have seen, we each have an incredible capacity to access inspiration and to inspire others, working with them to give structure to our projects. So why aren't we all living inspired and creative lives? This is because most of us are subject to resistance, which is where we are going to turn our attention next…

PART TWO: YOUR POWER TO OVERCOME RESISTANCE

CHAPTER 4:
YOUR POWER TO UNDERSTAND RESISTANCE

'Every sun casts a shadow, and genius's shadow is resistance. As powerful as is our soul's call to realisation, so potent are the forces of resistance arrayed against it.'

Steven Pressfield, The War of Art

Welcome to inspiration's 'evil twin' – resistance. Really inspired about your next action? Cue resistance. Resistance comes in many forms and acts as a barrier to creative fulfilment. Your decision to respond to your calling and offer your leadership will probably be met with a lot of internal resistance and fear. In fact, inspiration might well lead you into a direct confrontation with precisely your *greatest* fears and *deepest-seated* resistance – not, I believe, to scare or punish you, but to move you beyond these. Inspired leadership is not about waving a magic wand to overcome obstacles, but about learning how to do the work we were born to do, even, and especially, in the face of resistance.

Cue Resistance – a Terrifying 'Plug-In!'

As I know from personal experience, resistance can show up in many ways. Even something seemingly tiny can open the floodgates to our inner resistance; however, this reminds us that resistance is fundamentally a product of our minds, not an attribute of external projects or actions. It has probably been there all the time, but only surfaces when we are taking a step towards acting on our inspiration.

I experienced this phenomenon in a recent coaching session with Roger. Alongside his successful corporate career in events management, Roger had been working on a personal-development project that was much closer to his heart. In our last session, I had suggested that he should make a shift from preparing his project to launching it at a small public event; to prove the concept, you might say. He was excited by the idea and I was looking forward to hearing his progress since we last spoke.

When we reconvened, Roger said he'd had a really inspiring conversation with a potential client, and that his wife had remarked how alive he seemed. However, he then went on to explain that he had done hardly anything to organise the actual event. He had spoken to a web developer who was going to work with him on it, and she explained that she'd love to do it, but she needed him to buy four 'plug-ins' – enabling pieces of software code. So Roger had gone online to buy the plug-ins, got his credit card out, and then ended up not buying any of them.

He had stalled.

'I just couldn't do it!' he explained. 'It meant I would actually make this thing real!' He said he felt ashamed of himself, and as if he wanted to abandon the whole thing. His self-doubt was up, big time. I sincerely hoped he would be able to find his way again and free himself from the harmful story he was telling himself.

Roger told me that he couldn't believe that simply contemplating clicking on 'buy now' and spending a few pounds could bring up so much fear in him. It was obviously not the act itself, but the potential meaning of the act that had triggered so much fear and self-criticism for him.

I reassured him that there was nothing wrong with him, and that he had simply stumbled into the painful threshold of resistance. This was all *part* of the journey to his self-actualisation, not a hindrance to it. I had every faith that he could get through it. I had been around the block enough times myself to know that these dust storms of resistance, however big they seem and bad they feel, usually herald a breakthrough of some kind and can mark the start of a new chapter. In mythological terms, he was experiencing an 'all hope is lost' moment – the darkest point before dawn (see page 164).

Although Roger could grasp the concept of resistance logically, he was obviously very caught up in his emotional experience of it. The following week, he said, 'It's clear to me that the issue isn't really the plug-ins, as we discussed; it's the much deeper fear of fully committing to what I want to create... But the plug-ins discussion helped me find the courage to call my new web developer and tell her exactly what was going on for me – including the fear, paralysis and shame, and even the fact that I'd sat at my computer on several occasions to buy the plug-ins, but just couldn't bring myself do it. It was a great conversation and has brought a new calm to the myriad of feelings I'd been having about my project.'

But he still hadn't bought the plug-ins.

Because Roger had become immersed in the emotional experience of resistance, thinking alone probably wouldn't have helped him shift into action. He needed me to temporarily go there with him, empathise and show compassion, and then help him lead himself gently back to his creative power to take the actions he was initially terrified to take.

We often stall and feel like giving up just when things are about to get good. Thankfully, Roger didn't take this as a sign that he shouldn't be pursuing his project. Instead, he came to realise that any step could awaken his demons of resistance. He just didn't see it coming, like most of us don't. Suddenly we find ourselves deep in resistance, wondering, 'What the hell just happened?'

So what did Robert do next? I asked him if he could buy just the one plug-in for now, then see how he felt afterwards. He said he would do that and took the next step in his journey.

Here is what I have come to recognise as a rule of thumb: the more important an action or a project is to you and your leadership evolution, the more resistance you are likely to experience to following through on it. The area of life that brings you the most discomfort shows where you're likely to be ripe for growth.

I think that many of us initially believe that following our inspiration should be easy and that one day we'll just march off into the sunset in pursuit of it. As a result, we think there is something wrong with us when it turns out to be harder than we anticipated. While we want to remain positive, negativity and fears start creeping in; and we grow alarmed and believe that something must be wrong. This anxiety is really important to acknowledge when it comes to the effects of resistance.

My experience is that many of our creative and leadership gifts are never fully expressed, or expressed at all, because we meet our inner resistance and subsequently talk ourselves out of realising them. These gifts might remain in our minds, hearts and hard drives, but not where they belong – expressed in the world.

'Buy' Inspiration, Get Resistance Free

Inspiration and resistance operate as a double act, a package. You can't receive inspiration without resistance automatically making an uninvited appearance at some point. On the positive side, this means that resistance acts like a secondary force; it only arises *because* you get inspired, and you are in the vicinity of your purpose in life. Something stirred in you.

It's interesting that inspiration is sometimes likened to a bolt of lightning. We know that the appearance of lightning usually heralds the arrival of the thunder. So it is with inspiration. Once we are inspired, the rumbles of resistance are very likely to follow. The key is the meaning we give to resistance. We may see resistance as evidence that we are weak or that we have failed; or even that there is something very wrong about what we are doing. Some people even believe their resistance is a form of punishment for daring to act on their dreams, or that it's a malignant force of some sort.

The truth is that resistance is our ego's fearful response to the creative leadership impulses of our soul. It tries to keep us small and afraid to prevent us from fulfilling our purpose in life. I see resistance as residing in the egotistic part of the mind that focuses on material existence and earning approval; it wants us to believe our role in life is primarily to avoid failure, criticism and judgement.

I, for one, grew up thinking that if I was afraid to move in a particular direction in life, then I should go in another direction that didn't seem so scary. Today, I believe the complete opposite: the presence of resistance is usually a sign that you are facing in the right direction in your life, and you can lean into it and discover the gift waiting for you.

Personally, I like to think that resistance is evidence that we are dreaming boldly. While the experience of resistance can be difficult, we can come to look on resistance as a gift and a pointer. The fact that you experience so much resistance to an action or a project is usually an indication that the action is highly important for your leadership evolution. It is a measure of your 'repressed' inspiration, passion and love and how much energy you actually have for your project.

The presence of resistance is usually evidence that there is something *to* resist. Resistance is like the distorted echo of inspiration. When you get clear on what you are resisting, you are likely to be clear on your next step or steps. Like the actor who doesn't want to play the role again that they have already mastered, you want to lean in to your resistance, so you can expand, learn and grow, and discover the gift it is trying to hide from you.

A Sleeper Cell Awoken

What elicits resistance? As we have seen, resistance is most likely to appear when you are on the threshold of a significant action, project or shift in thinking and about to step into a new, authentic chapter of creativity, leadership and power. Until then, it is there but lying dormant like a sleeper cell. No matter what form it takes, it really means that at some level you are resisting becoming the person you were born to be; you are resisting the call of inspiration and with it the opportunity for success and a wonderfully creative life, experiencing just how amazing you really can be.

Resistance is likely to show up around one of the following:

- Soon after you get truly inspired – at the conception point of a new project.
- When you are about to take a step in order to progress, to finish or ship and share your work with the world.
- When you are on the verge of an important change.
- When a new chapter is beckoning you.
- When you want to move into a more real, purposeful and authentic expression of who you are.
- When you are about to step into self-leadership.

The older I get, the more in awe I am that anything gets created at all. We all seem to be up against so much in ourselves.

Are We All Subject to Resistance?

As far as I can tell, the vast majority of us experience resistance. I used to think it was just me, my guilty secret, my secret shame. Everyone else seemed to find things easy, and just get on with life. I was the scared one who dragged his heels. I felt like I had a character defect, and was especially flawed and useless. I knew what I wanted to do, yet I just didn't get on and do it.

Now, having had hundreds of conversations with all sorts of people around the world at all stages of their lives and careers, I think if we are really honest with ourselves, we all experience resistance, and we each have our own particular flavours of it. Even though you may feel like you personally qualify for a gold medal in resistance, I'm afraid this doesn't make you special. When it comes to resistance, we are all gold medallists.

How I Resist

The very activities we resist the most actively are often the areas of endeavour that may well hold the most fruitfulness for you. That has certainly been the case for me. Each area of my success – writing, speaking, coaching, publishing, broadcasting and teaching – has been preceded by degrees of resistance, from mild to moderate and at times severe, and even chronic 'give up and die' kinds of resistance. But as I have continually leaned in to my resistance, I have learned to embrace the gifts that resistance was trying to hide from me.

Here are a few of my favourite forms of resistance, which might strike a chord with you too: I procrastinate; I rationalise ideas away and convince myself how they could never work; I avoid things; I tell myself that I am not ready yet; I keep going on other people's courses and programmes; I keep studying other people's work; I doubt myself and judge myself; I tell myself nobody wants to hear what I have to say and that other people have better things to say than I do. I invest more in other people's success than my own. I continually compare myself to others unfavourably.

And What About You…?

I used to think that 'successful' people didn't experience resistance; somehow they were either lucky to be free of it, or had found some sort of magic formula to overcome it. My gradual realisation over the years has been this: that 'successful' people experience resistance too; they have simply been courageous enough to keep going in the face of it.

That we have resistance is not really the issue. How we relate to it and act when confronted by it is more important. But first of all we have to recognise it. Take a look at the following list and make a note of how many of this fit your own experience:

1. Dismissing inspired ideas out of hand.
2. Convincing yourself, albeit with apparently logical reasons, why your idea will never work.
3. Procrastination and delay.
4. Self-sabotaging behaviours.
5. Planning and over-preparing, but not executing.
6. Not showing up authentically in your work at all.
7. Thinking big but acting small.

8. Editing modifying or adapting yourself and how you show up.
9. Excessive emotional drama.
10. Becoming a perpetual student – reading and studying rather than doing.
11. Being overly controlling
12. Perfectionism.

These are some of the surface symptoms of resistance, which can often hide the deeper conditioning and the emotional turmoil that's going on in our minds.

Over-Preparation as a Form of Resistance

Sarah had approached me about coaching over a number of years, yet she had never got round to it. This time she told me, 'I really am ready!' So she paid me in advance to coach her for a year as a sign of her commitment to her personal growth at this point in her life.

At sixty, she was the MD of her own care company, which she was preparing to sell so she could focus on a new project. This idea was about empowering women between the ages of forty-five and seventy to claim their own authentic voice. Yet Sarah could become so easily distracted. We would be clear about her next steps in one session, but her clarity seemed to have completely disappeared by the time we spoke again. She'd usually explain she had been very busy, so hadn't made any progress. In one session, she reported having re-read her favourite book on leadership for the sixth time to refresh her thinking. While I'm sure there was some value in re-reading the book, I couldn't help but think there would be greater value in taking action on her own project.

She was still waiting for that magical day that she would wake up feeling confident enough to start. She was also a perfectionist, so I helped her see that while her high standards were important, things didn't need to be absolutely perfect. She was her own worst critic and forever battling with the voice in her head that said she wasn't good enough and she needed to prepare more. At the age of sixty, she was also struggling with the idea of being a 'beginner' again.

My antidote was to keep encouraging her to start small and to try out her fledgling wings as she went. She had given talks but hadn't charged for this, so when she got her first paying client, this was very significant for her. It got her over the threshold of earning her first income from a coaching session. She 'proved' the concept.

Another client, Alex, had created all his content but had not yet gone 'live' by sharing his work with the world. He kept getting caught up in trivial stuff. I shared an image with him of a shopkeeper who kept fiddling about with his stock but who still had the 'closed' sign up, even though there was a queue of people waiting for him to turn over the sign to say 'open'. Alex was terrified to open for business, even though people were practically banging on his door, wanting his help.

Most of us have no idea just how inspiring or helpful we could be to other people right now, if only we followed our inspiration and got our ideas out into the world.

Resistance, Reality and Intuition

I occasionally have clients who use resistance as yet another reason to be tough on themselves. Although sometimes it's not just about resistance. Sometimes it's just the reality of life – we all have commitments and a lot on our plates. We might be ill; we might have young children or aging parents or demanding bosses; or sometimes we are simply exhausted and overwhelmed by life.

At other times, it might be that our intuition is guiding us away from a particular course of action, because it's not right for us in some way, or at least not at the moment. Sometimes, it's OK to come to terms with being inspired by a project, yet simply not having the time or energy to follow through on it.

However, there is a big difference between forcing ourselves to do something that really isn't for us, versus overcoming the resistance to do what we are truly inspired to do and would love to do. I think part of the journey for each of us is being able to discern the subtle differences between resistance and intuition. So how to tell the difference between them?

When my clients are facing this dilemma, there are a couple of factors that I ask them to consider:

- Did you feel truly inspired, and then within seconds, minutes, hours or days, the doubts, fears and rationalisations began to creep in – and you slow down or even stop? That is likely to be resistance insidiously creeping in.
- Alternatively, has something never felt quite right, and perhaps you've never really felt inspired? However, you thought you should be or ought to follow through nevertheless, and managed you talk yourself into it with a heavy heart? That could well be the result of trying to override the voice of your intuition.

What is the Cost of Not Acknowledging Resistance?

I once had a conversation with a woman who worked in IT, who had developed a programme to help parents keep their children safe online by spotting potential abusers rather than genuine connections. It seemed a truly helpful programme to get out in to the world, and she even had a potential collaborator lined up who could help market it. But she kept saying to me, 'I don't know what is wrong with me and why I'm not moving forward.'

I explained the concept of resistance to her, and how, in my experience, it was an almost inevitable part of the creative leadership journey. But it just didn't seemed to resonate with her, at least not at that time. As far as I know, her important programme never got launched and the good it could do was never realised.

When we remain oblivious to resistance, this doesn't mean we have managed to avoid it. Instead, it probably keeps operating, but just out of our awareness. Then we can feel like we are caught in our own inertia or like we are forever battling something or somebody. Really, we are battling aspects of ourselves. We feel held back, playing smaller than we can; wondering if we are capable of more, but not finding out. Or we may just beat ourselves up about it.

Other People's Resistance

It is bad enough that we have our own resistance, but it's often fed by the fears and lousy advice of other people. However, while we can be crushed by what other people say to us, it can also fuel us to prove them wrong and demonstrate what we are capable of.

I recently met Harry, who was on the team that produced the recording of the song *'Bohemian Rhapsody'* by Queen. He laughed as he told me that the record company executives refused at first to release a pop song that was six minutes long. Then radio DJ Kenny Everett got hold of a copy of the song and played it, generating an overwhelming public response. So the record company capitulated, the song was released and went on to become a hit and one of the most iconic songs of all time. Naturally, the company then expressed how much faith they had always had in it!

My friend Liz was told by her mum as a child, 'No one will ever be interested in what you have to say.' She is now a TV producer and, as I mentioned earlier, the Executive Producer of *Downton Abbey*.

Similarly, when my friend Louis was fifteen, he picked up a guitar for the first time. Immediately, his uncle told him not to waste his time and money on playing the guitar. Yes, he was spending more time on his guitar than on his school studies, but within two years Louis was playing guitar on TV with the likes of Rod Stewart and Chuck Berry. He went on to support the Rolling Stones and other successful bands, travel the world and become a highly respected bass player.

Thank God he didn't listen to his uncle.

I think we need to understand the good intentions of people who seem to want to undermine us or hold us back.

They care about us. They don't want to see us screw up our lives and end up suffering. But often they don't have any experience in our areas of interest, so they can't give relevant advice because they simply don't know the facts. When we are exploring new areas, we may have enough of our own doubts and fears, and don't need theirs too!

We are all up against a lot – both from within ourselves and from the people around us. How rich the world is when we manage to ignore our own and other people's opinions, and how much richer it can still become as we beat our resistance to show up with more of our gifts.

But that isn't to say that everyone else's advice is rubbish. One of the significant elements of maturity is being able to discern the quality of advice being offered to us. As the mystic poet Rumi wrote: 'When embarking upon an adventure, do not consult someone who has never left home!'

How wise that is.

Illuminating Resistance

Unfortunately, identifying resistance doesn't mean it just goes away! Resistance largely operates out of our conscious awareness, which is how it maintains its grip on us. Yet as we illuminate it, bring to the light and start to see its dynamics clearly, we're no longer inclined to treat it as a character defect on our part, but something universal that we are all dealing with to some extent or another.

When I first went into therapy in 1986, I thought I just needed to throw a little light on one or two issues, but as I got in deeper, I didn't like what I saw! I thought, 'I'm not in need of a little tweaking, I am actually totally screwed!' I felt like Private Fraser, the character in *Dad's Army* who keeps saying, 'We're doomed!' I don't feel like that now – but I know that sometimes when we initially throw light on something that we have hidden away, things can look even worse for a while. When we realise we've only been considering the tip of the iceberg, and that beyond it lies a whole iceberg, our hearts may sink.

However, this is when we need to say to ourselves: 'Precisely because this is scary, it probably means it's right for me!' I call this 'resisting with awareness'. It means a life of fulfilment as a result of moving through fears and resistance; whereas resistance causes so many of us to live lives slightly parallel to our true calling.

In the next chapter, we are going to explore how to shift out of the shadows and show up in the power of that calling.

CHAPTER 5
YOUR POWER TO COME OUT OF THE SHADOWS

'Sometimes, when we are terrified of embracing our true calling, we'll pursue a shadow calling instead. That shadow career is a metaphor for our real career. Its shape is similar, its contour tantalising the same. But a shadow career entails no risk.'

Steven Pressfield, *Turning Pro*

Living a shadow life is one way in which resistance can manifest itself.

Gary had been immersed in the area of men's health and wellbeing for over twenty-five years, mainly on the systems and IT side. His tech role enabled men to access the support, ideas and information that would help them when they felt desperate and even suicidal. This was his world; it was where he belonged.

However, he increasingly wondered whether he might have his own voice on the subject, with something valid to say. He came to me for coaching so that he could discover what his own voice might be. As we worked together to unearth his experience and the wisdom he had developed, he became inspired – and his resistance was triggered. Although he created some new content, he kept feeding his resistance by looking at what other men were offering, and usually ended up feeling deflated and disheartened as a result. He doubted he had anything unique to say or that anyone would really want to listen to him. He was unsure whether he could create his own successful business around what he wanted to teach. His inner critic surfaced with vengeance.

For him, thinking too far ahead became a form of resistance which mean he remained in his shadow life. He ended up feeling flat and uninspired because he then moved away from what had initially really inspired him to a compromise he thought might make money for him. By trying to solve future problems rather than tackle current problems, he kept diluting his power in the present moment.

What Your Own Shadow Life Might Look Like

'Are you getting your PhD in Elizabethan studies because you are afraid to write your own tragedies and comedies that you know you have inside you? Are you living the drugs-and-booze half of the musician's life, without actually making the music? Are you working for an innovator because you are afraid to risk becoming an innovator yourself?'

Steven Pressfield, *Turning Pro*

We have seen how resistance doesn't want us to follow our true calling, and scares us with fears about what might go wrong if we were to take the next step. It can likewise hijack creativity and channel it so that we end up living a shadow life! But how can you tell if that's the case for you? You might be living a show life if you find yourself...

- supporting the talent of others, rather than acknowledging and developing your own talents;
- denying that you even have any talent of your own and insisting only others have talent;
- immersing yourself in, or weighing yourself down with, other people's problems;
- being jealous and critical of others for doing what secretly you haven't had the courage to do, as they remind you of your unfulfilled dreams and unlived life;
- being public and showing up, but for a cause that isn't close to your own heart and isn't authentically you;
- beavering away on your creative projects in private, but never putting them out for public scrutiny;
- playing safe with the projects you are given, rather than initiating projects that feel more inspiring, exciting and scary for you;

- focusing on the mundane and less risky parts of your business rather than the cutting edge, where you'd really make a difference;
- believing that your identity and credibility originate from the kudos of working for a prestigious company rather than for yourself – and that you'd be nothing on your own;
- getting your significance by association, such as who you know, who you work with, who your friends are;
- always thinking that you are 'less than' others and habitually putting yourself down;
- trying to force yourself to be grateful – when in your heart you know it's time to graduate to something bigger and more exciting;
- continually distracting yourself so as to avoid what excites and scares you;
- compulsively trying to please others and meeting what you believe are their expectations of you, whilst potentially neglecting your own needs;
- trying to get everyone else to change, or be more creative, even demanding they change, when the invitation is for you to change and show up more;
- waiting to be discovered rather than making yourself discoverable;
- getting into fights, arguments and power struggles with other people, which then keep you distracted and stuck;
- losing yourself in some kind of addiction.

Do We All Live Shadow Lives?

I wonder if living some kind of shadow life is an almost inevitable and even necessary chapter of our leadership evolution. Why do I think it is inevitable? In my three decades of travelling the world, it has become clear to me that relatively few of us have been actively encouraged, let alone actively supported, in finding our true calling – what we were 'born to do' in my terminology. Consequently, we feel like something is missing and are drawn as if magnetically to the *area* of our true calling. However, we then play a 'smaller' role in that area, living in the shadows of our true calling.

A 'shadow interest' means an area of interest, passion and curiosity which you love and enjoy being around, but where you never quite put your own talent out there fully. For example, you might dream of writing a book, so you go to work in a shop where you are surrounded by books, you can buy books at discount, meet people every day who love books and sometimes you get to meet authors too. On one level your passion is being fed, and it can look like you are living the dream, but on another level, your calling goes hungry. The truth is, you might still be resisting and hiding out because you are not writing your own book.

Moving out of the shadows and following the path of our true calling is, in my experience, a courageous act of self-leadership.

From Echo to Authenticity

UK comedian and actress Victoria Wood once said in an interview: 'Until you find your voice, you are just echoing what has gone before.' As shadow artists, we will likely start to learn our craft by echoing what has gone before, but if we persevere, we will discover that we actually have something authentic, unique and interesting to express ourselves. This is an important part of the journey.

There can be a sort of mysterious osmotic effect that happens when we regularly immerse ourselves in the inspiration offered by others. It can awaken the seeds that are already innate within us but have so far lain dormant. You have probably heard of seeds that lie dormant in the desert until the rain falls and then they germinate. Some seeds can remain this way for decades, even centuries. But the potential in the seeds is always there. They are just waiting for the right conditions, a the right nutrients, so that they can fulfil that latent potential. When the rain comes they blossom, however long they have been sleeping.

You are the same. There are seeds within you that may have lain dormant your whole life, or, if you believe it, over many lifetimes. And now you can eventually create the right conditions for your blossoming to happen. Validation and a sense of possibility are two of the key nutrients you may need to awaken those seeds. Being around inspiration and immersing yourself in it will also act as a nutrient for the seeds in your soul, and those seeds – your gifts – which have lain dormant – start to germinate and come to life. With the right circumstances, internally and externally, you will begin to find your voice, your own natural style and your unique ways of creating.

However, as we have seen, once we do find our own way of expressing ourselves, many of us still feel trapped in self-judgement. We are overly invested in judging ourselves rather than in creating. That's why I believe a shadow life can actually be a successful pointer to our true calling, when we have an expanded awareness. The danger is that we might get stuck in it, not realising that inspiration is inviting us to graduate from it.

My Own Shadow Life

By 1997, I'd been involved with Alternatives for nine years, and co-running it for two years, when I learned an important lesson about my own shadow life. Alternatives is an independent, not-for-profit organisation dedicated to raising awareness. In many respects, I was 'living the dream' by working there and being immersed in the area of personal and spiritual growth, having left the corporate world. There I was, co-running the top weekly platform in London and getting to meet and be inspired by some of the leading names in the field, such as Deepak Chopra, Wayne Dyer, Marianne Williamson, Eckhart Tolle, Neale Donald Walsh, Susan Jeffers, Shakti Gawain and Robert Bly, as well as many lesser known but equally high-quality authors and speakers. Although I had successfully given some few talks and workshops myself, I hadn't yet started to write a book.

Yet increasingly, I could hear a nagging voice at the back of my mind. I was getting a bit bored, perhaps, and found myself making judgements about some of the speakers, along the lines of: 'I've heard that before. That's not new; even I could tell people about that.' I tried to ignore the feeling and told myself I should be grateful for the position I had, but secretly I feared that maybe my dream wasn't the right one after all; either that or – yes – there really must be something wrong with me, falling into a familiar pattern of self-blame. There I was, living the dream, and still not happy! Was I never going to be happy?

I went on holiday to Lanzarote with my partner, Helen, and I took with me Julia Cameron's book *The Artist's Way*, which several people had recommended to me. Ostensibly, I took the book so that I could type up some of the great insights it contained for my growing collection of inspirational quotations. As I was flicking through it, though, I started to read the text more closely and was drawn in particular to a short section about 'the shadow artist'.

As I read through those few paragraphs, I was shocked by how Cameron described the shadow artist:

Shadow artists often choose shadow careers – those close to the desired art, even parallel to it, but not the art itself... As a rule of thumb, shadow artists judge themselves harshly, beating themselves for years over the fact they have not acted on their dreams. This cruelty only reinforces their status as shadow artists.

I had what I now affectionately call an 'oh shit!' moment. That was me! I had come such a long way, but it suddenly occurred to me that I was *still* living a shadow life. My situation looked great: there I was, supporting these inspiring and creative souls, frequently leaders in their fields, and marketing and organising talks for them that often sold out. But then it hit me: I didn't want to be the organising talks for speakers any more. I really wanted to be the speaker. I didn't just want to support authors; I was inspired to become an author myself. I didn't want to support thought-leaders; I wondered whether I might become one myself. It was time for me to graduate to the next stage in my life.

For a moment, I felt clear, uplifted and inspired – but it didn't last long. My resistance kicked in and I suddenly started to feel scared and vulnerable again. I couldn't see how I would ever make a living from speaking, writing and coaching. The gap between where I wanted to be and where I was now seemed too massive to bridge. And who would want to listen to me or read my books when there were already so many other eloquent people out there? What was special or different about me? Would I find a place in the world if I wasn't leading Alternatives, which had been my spiritual home for years?

Co-leading Alternatives had been a wonderful training ground, but there was a new chapter waiting for me – or at least I hoped there was! Although I had been very visible in my work, introducing events in front of 700 people at times, I was also hiding out. However, I still felt very uncomfortable about investing in my own success. It was much more comfortable living vicariously – investing in the success of others.

All the same, I could no longer deny that by promoting other speakers, I was running away from my own voice. By hosting other writers, I was running away from my own impulse to write. I was more at ease helping others to shine than stepping up and revealing my own light. I wasn't facing my own demons. I was fleeing from the calling that inspiration was inviting me to accept. Yet try as I might, I couldn't go back to being *unaware.* I realised my job was to awaken more of my own inspiration, not just to admire the messages and leadership of others.

The Three Things that Help Us Graduate

There are three pro-active steps you can take to support your transition from a shadow life to your true calling:

1. Invest in yourself and your projects – over and again

Commit to yourself and your projects – and keep that commitment going. When I had that initial moment of insight, I started a writing practice. The key difference was I started to write regularly and consistently, whether I felt like it or not, rather than just when I was in the mood, which had been my previous habit. As I devoted myself to regular writing, I found the Muse seemed to smile on me and my commitments, and give me more things to write about.

2. Put yourself forward

Quit waiting to be discovered; it might never happen! Instead, venture to put yourself out there. Within a year of deciding how I wanted my life to change, I had submitted a book proposal to several leading UK publishers. I was willing to believe in myself, even in the face of resistance and my inner critic. I began to champion myself and become bolder and more audacious on my own behalf. I also started to put myself forward for more teaching and speaking opportunities, and more doors began to open for me. A publisher offered me a contract and my first book was published in 1999.

3. Develop a new relationship with resistance

There might never be a moment when you feel you are completely ready. Act anyway. I secretly harboured a hope that one day I would wake up feeling more confident, capable and significant, but that day never came. So I decided to go ahead despite this, in the face of my resistance rather than waiting for resistance to subside. I realised this *was* my life – continually being plagued by resistance and insecurity, and choosing to go ahead and do my work anyway. I turned pro: I loved the work so much that I wanted to make speaking, writing, coaching, publishing and broadcasting messages the centre of my professional life, not leave them on the edge of it.

How to Make the Shift from Your Shadow Life to Your True Calling

We all have a lived life and an as-yet unlived life. If we wish to move from our shadow selves into our true selves, the first stage is to become aware of what has been going on and to face this with compassion. Most shadow artists are afraid to put their creativity at the centre of their own lives, and we need to be honest about this, and not to beat ourselves up mercilessly for having done it.

Likewise, we need to avoid making excuses for how we've been hiding out. In his essay 'Self-Reliance', the American writer Ralph Waldo Emerson states: 'In every work of genius we recognise our own rejected thoughts; they come back to us with a certain alienated majesty.' It's natural to think 'I could have done that' when we connect with a work that speaks to us in some way. However, the issue isn't so much about 'Could you?' as 'Will you?' In essence, you are an incredibly powerful being. To me, that is a given. The real question is: 'Will you follow your talent to all the places it might take you?'

- To make the shift from your shadow self to your True Self, and to follow where inspiration leads, there are some simple steps you can put into practice:
- Recognise that you do have an unlived life – and that you want to live more of it.
- Acknowledge, accept and begin to change the core negative beliefs that you harbour about yourself.
- Take yourself more seriously – and accept that you are in some way creative.
- Give yourself permission to blossom and fulfil your latent potential.
- Commit to your own creativity by cultivating daily creative practices.
- Listen to, trust and follow your inspiration.
- Start saying no to people and opportunities where necessary, if these aren't the right fit for your True Self.
- Become a better friend to yourself, kinder and less critical.
- Become bolder and more audacious on your own behalf, taking affirmative action rather than getting caught up in other people's unhelpful judgements or demands.

Changing Your Relationship with Your Inner Critic

'As a rule of thumb, shadow artists judge themselves harshly, beating themselves for years over the years they have not acted on their dreams. This cruelty only reinforces their status as shadow artists. Remember it takes nurturing to make an artist. Shadow artists did not receive sufficient nurturing. They blame themselves for not acting fearlessly anyhow.'

Julia Cameron, *The Artist's Way*

Despite our best intentions, we might stay stuck as shadow artists. Either we don't show up, or we don't show up as powerfully as we might, because we are at the mercy of our inner critic, or fear the criticism that others aim at us. We don't feel safe or protected so we continue hiding out and playing smaller than we could.

As far as I can tell, we each have an inner critic, which judges us at every stage of our creative journeys. I am not sure we can ever get rid of it; in fact, even trying to get rid of it can somehow give it strength and feed it by making it more real. When we are motivated largely by our inner critic we might achieve a lot, but we won't necessarily feel good about our achievements, which won't seem that meaningful.

However, while we might not be able to rid ourselves completely of our inner critic, we can shrink its hold over us. We can do this by developing a different relationship with it that enables us to take it less seriously and to see it for the uncreative, shaming and controlling bully that it is. We can also develop an inner champion to oppose it.

A Tip for Dealing with Your Inner Critic
Julia Cameron has a great tip for loosening the grip of your inner critic. She dealt with hers by externalising it and using humour to dissolve its power. She gave her inner critic a name and a persona – she called it Nigel, and decided he was an interior designer! Whenever she was writing something and her inner critic began to kick

in, she would e-mail her editor, and explain, 'Look, I have been writing this and Nigel is telling me its rubbish, so would you have a look and tell me what you think?'

Developing an Inner Champion

Where the inner critic is about seeing ourselves through the eyes of judgement, the inner champion is about seeing ourselves through the eyes of love and acceptance. The inner champion allows us to see ourselves more clearly, to know our good qualities and our immense potential, and also to recognise our weaknesses. Nevertheless it remains supportive, validating and encouraging.

Sadly, many of us didn't grow up surrounded by other people who championed us and our creative power. Our inner artist was not nourished, and instead often shamed or ignored. As a consequence, we might be hungry for validation; there are things we longed to hear when we were young that we never heard, and a part of us still yearns to hear them. A few words of support, encouragement and validation from others can go a very long way. When we develop our own inner champion, we can carry that voice with us wherever we go.

To develop your own inner champion, take action:

1. Accept your inner critic – don't deny or fight it. Much of what it says probably doesn't come from you anyway: it is the internalised voice of your parents, siblings, teachers, colleagues and other influences. It might even be part of your ancestry, passed down your generational line.
2. Show compassion for yourself and the pain the inner critic might cause you.
3. Work on your self-care, self-nurture and self-encouragement.
4. Be kind to yourself.
5. Surround yourself with positive and encouraging people who act like 'believing mirrors', reflecting back all that's good about you.

6. Quarantine the amount of time you spend with other people who are excessively critical of you or themselves.
7. Listen to your inner champion when you have every reason to celebrate your success.

Showing Up Versus Showing Off

'Shadow artists gravitate towards their rightful tribe but cannot yet claim their birth right… they are hiding in the shadows, afraid to expose the dream to the light, fearful that it will disintegrate to the touch.'

Julia Cameron, *The Artist's Way*

In my work over the years, I've discovered that many of us resonate strongly with the problem of showing up versus showing off. It lies at the heart of why many of us end up living shadow lives. As part of our conditioning, we have received messages along the lines of *don't show off, don't draw attention to yourself* and *don't speak too highly of yourself.* We internalise these messages in the form of our inner critic. In this way, our ego hijacks our healthy desire to show up in the world and play our part, judging us harshly for daring to act on this impulse. As a result, many of us spend our whole lives worrying about being labelled as a show off, to the extent that we rarely let ourselves truly show up. We rob the world of the best of us.

Showing up, though, I think is one of the most generous things we can do. Our playing smaller than we truly are doesn't serve us or the world. When we show up, we inspire others, we shine our light and we get past our fears. In essence, the last three decades of my own life have been learning how to show up in the world authentically, and clearing the blocks to do doing that. It is the major work I do with most of my coaching clients too – encouraging and inspiring them to show up powerfully and authentically in their lives.

When we were young we probably weren't often told we were creative, so our latent creativity manifests itself by drawing us to the creative force field of others, while we stay on the edge of our own power. This offers a degree of satisfaction, but we will never be deeply fulfilled until we let our own leadership and creativity see the light of day.

Permission to Be Bold

For many of us, championing ourselves doesn't come naturally. We creatives often struggle to speak highly of ourselves and our work, and secretly wish we had a manager, agent, benefactor or patron who could toot our horn for us. When we are given opportunities, we fulfil them admirably, but when it comes to creating opportunities for ourselves, we don't find it so easy.

A friend of mine is a very accomplished and capable actor; he refers to it as his calling. He has worked with many other great household name actors and done some fantastic work on stage, TV and in films. In the '80s and '90s he was in constant demand. But today, he feels quite underutilised. While he keeps himself busy with his family and domestic life, he isn't getting to do the work he truly loves. While this is usual in the world of acting, there was also a deeper dynamic at work.

Much of Nigel's earlier work had come to him through the agents he'd had over the years. Increasingly the world has changed, though, and younger actors are now putting themselves up for parts without the help of agents. They hear which productions are coming up, contact the casting director direct and showcase themselves directly. Nigel could see what was happening and what he needed to do, yet he found it hard to shift into self-championing mode. He was doing it, but it didn't come naturally, and I really felt for him. It can often seem that the world rewards those who make the most noise, rather than the most talented.

Cultivating Spiritual Audacity

I have come to embrace the word 'audacious'. I don't always find it an easy quality to embody, even though when I do act audaciously, good and interesting things tend to follow as a consequence. As Julia Cameron rightly says in *The Artist's Way*, what makes the difference is not our talent alone, but being audacious and bold on behalf of ourselves and our talent.

Let's be clear. Audacity differs greatly from obnoxiousness, which is ego-driven and largely self-serving. I am particularly drawn to the idea of audacious expressions of love. I remember hearing the spiritual author and teacher Marianne Williamson talk at Alternatives about hate, terrorism and prejudice – and how the propagators of these are often much more audacious, committed and focused than those of us who want to stand for a more loving and fairer world. She was calling for the rest of us to take an even more audacious stand for love in the world, which is a very powerful and inspiring message.

The Uniqueness of You

By 2002 I had stepped back from the day to day running of Alternatives for a couple of years, but was still on the board of trustees. I'd two books published by then, with a third on its way. Alternatives invited me to be part of a panel of events in a series called *Publish Your Book*. They ran the event six times, during which there was a particular question that we members of the panel kept being asked over and again by attendees, albeit in different ways:

> *What have I got to say that hasn't already been said, and probably said by people better qualified or more articulate than me?*

This was a question I asked myself many times when I was coming out of the shadows of my own life. I had a deep empathy with those who asked it, so I took time to meditate on it. I didn't want to offer a glib answer, but an answer that I could truly believe in and stand behind. After some time, this is the response I came up with:

> *We are individual expressions of universal ideas. Our job is not to try to manufacture difference, but to reveal our pre-*

existing uniqueness. We are each a unique corner of creation, here to allow and value our authentic expression. On a spiritual level, there is no competition to be you.

I truly believe this. It is my advice to all artists, creatives, leaders and entrepreneurs: be yourself and allow more of yourself out into the world. Don't try to manufacture some persona that you hope and think might work, because even if it does, you will probably feel you have sold out on yourself. When we have lost touch with our True Self and have come to believe that we are not enough or are inadequate in some way, it is very tempting to think we need to play roles.

A Unique Take on Ancient Ideas

Although I stepped down from being a trustee of Alternatives in 2009, I have stayed a part of the wider Alternatives community, and recently attended a day-long event with internationally acclaimed Buddhist teacher and author Jack Kornfield.

The event was billed as 'The Buddhist Psychology of Self-Love and Self-Compassion' and around 500 people attended. While I was familiar with the concepts he was discussing, I found something about Jack's energy, experience, wisdom, humour and insight utterly compelling. The whole day was glorious. It deepened my understanding of these ancient ideas. Jack was teaching universal Buddhist ideas that were millennia old, but he didn't try to be different. Instead, by being fully himself, he was utterly unique and touched a spot in us all.

Don't Try to Manufacture Uniqueness – Reveal It

Uniqueness is an interesting idea. The ego part of ourselves usually tells us something like: *OK, I can see I need to make myself different. Say something that has never been said before. Set the world on fire with my idea. Have a novelty. I need to invent something unique.* We put pressure on ourselves to manufacture something that makes us stand out. And sometimes that works. But the problem is that every invention is likely to need a reinvention eventually. So we will then have to manufacture something else to retain public interest, more things that appear new and different. It can be very tiring, as well as often ineffective. We just add to the noise.

On a deeper level, as we have seen, you are already unique, and always have been. You were created unique. There is no competition to be you. There is a unique place for you to take up in life, a place you fit in to the whole of creation. You have gifts that you can express in your unique way. But so often these have been buried under roles and rules, shame, self-judgement and the belief that you are not 'enough'.

But here is what I have discovered: the more we allow our uniqueness out, the more we express ourselves humanely and authentically, the more resonance we are likely to create in the wider world. So in the next chapter we are diving in to how we get beyond our inner critic, beat our own resistance so we bring your projects and best qualities into the world.

CHAPTER 6
YOUR POWER TO BEAT RESISTANCE

'It's a terrible thing, I think, in life to wait until you're ready. I have this feeling now that actually no one is ever ready to do anything. There's almost no such thing as ready. There's only now. And you may as well do it now. I mean, I say that confidently as if I'm about to go bungee jumping or something – I'm not. I'm not a crazed risk taker. But I do think that, generally speaking, now is as good a time as any.'

Hugh Laurie, actor and musician

Jenny had 80 per cent finished her film, but had run out of funding. She felt ashamed and embarrassed, disheartened and a little deflated, like she was falling at the last hurdle. 'Should I give up or keep going?' was her question to me. I had no idea! I guessed resistance was at work, but wasn't sure what the way through for her was going to be. I sensed she was a bit trapped by her fear of failure, and also by her fear of success. A good recipe for staying stuck: damned if you do, damned if you don't.

It was clear that if she didn't complete the film, she would continue to feel bad about herself, and she would find it hard to start another project. Yet, knowing her a little, it seemed clear to me that she was born to make films. Film was an ideal canvas for her creative expression, and a way for her to inspire people and touch them emotionally. On top of this, she loved making them and was good at collaborating with others to get them made. She was a true artist.

We talked through the 'how to' and what remained for her to do to complete the film, how much more funding she would need, who she might approach for this funding, and then when and how she would launch her film. She understood her next steps, but I sensed there was still some resistance, so I asked her, 'And why would you go ahead and aim to finish your film?' I was hoping to help her open up to her sense of inspiration and positive possibility.

Jenny replied, 'I'll inspire myself and satisfy my curiosity about whether I can actually do this. I'll hate myself if I don't. If I were to complete it, I'd feel more confident about future projects. And who knows the positive impact I might be able to have on people through the film?' I could feel her energy rising and her sense of excitement increasing. She needed her 'why' to access the energy and fuel to follow through on the 'how'.

Next time we spoke, she told me that she had asked for and received the final tranche of funding and was close to completing the editing of the film, and was planning its release.

Her short film went on to become popular around the world and was shown at many international film festivals. Jenny received great critical acclaim as well as gratitude from people who watched the film and told her how its themes resonated with them. She also got to make another film about the making of the film. Her confidence increased massively, and doors opened to many more opportunities for her.

So the good news is that resistance is beatable. You can beat your resistance, if not immediately then over time. Every business, every work of art, every act of love, reconciliation, beauty and forgiveness is a testimony to a brave individual making something more important than their resistance. Personally, I don't think there is a 'resistance beating' gene that some of us have and some of us don't have. It is something we can all learn to do.

Reasons to Tackle Resistance

My conversations with Jenny brought home to me a crucial insight into getting beyond resistance. I had already spent a couple of decades exploring how people get past their resistance to show up with their leadership and creative gifts in the world. Now, though, I realised there is a crucial aspect that is often overlooked. Success is partly about *how* we get past our resistance, but we probably also need some compelling reasons as to *why* we should get past it.

As we have seen, often when we get caught up in resistance, we are at a threshold, a pivotal moment of choice. It can seem too scary, selfish or even impossible to carry on. At these times, it can seem like the easiest thing in the world to give up and the chances are that nobody else will even know that we ditched our project because of resistance. But we'll nevertheless feel bad about ourselves. Seeing the impact that Jenny's film had in the world and her own career, it became even clearer to me that when we give in to resistance, we rob ourselves and the world of our gifts.

So I am inviting you to go a little deeper into why you are inspired and committed to showing up in your life. Below are four ways to approach this: practical reasons, positive emotional reasons, 'negative' emotions, and then more spiritual/existential reasons why.

Write a list of your reasons in response to the following:

1. **Practical reasons:** e.g. 'showing up will increase my visibility, help me profile and get me more business.'
2. **Positive emotional reasons:** e.g. 'showing up makes me feel happy and alive; I feel most myself when I am showing up, sharing my gifts and contributing.'
3. **'Negative' emotional reasons:** e.g. 'I hate myself when I play small and let my fears defeat me, and I don't want to die with lots of regrets, knowing that so much of my music is still in me.'
4. **More 'Spiritual and existential' reasons:** e.g. 'I feel I am fulfilling my destiny when I show up; I feel inspired, *in spirit*, and I can feel the angels at my back cheering me on.'

Your reasons why will help you and others understand what you care about, and what your values are. Inspired leaders share their reasons why with the world. As you dive into this, it can also help you see what it is that you value more clearly, and what your true values are. Keep a list of these reasons to hand to help motivate you when things get tough, painful or whenever you feel helpless and hopeless.

Two Quick Tips for Overcoming Resistance
There is usually no mystery about what you need to do to continue or complete your creative and leadership projects. What is usually needed is one of two things:

1. Clarity about what your next small step could be and then accessing your inspiration and the courage to take that step.
2. Your reasons why you should take that step: your sense of motivation or the inspiration that fuels you to get beyond resistance and actually do the work.

Inspiration is a Necessity, Not a Luxury
I have often reflected on how many of our innate gifts lie dormant within each of us, and are never expressed. I have come to believe that sharing these gifts is essential for our own mental health and wellbeing. William Law, the eighteenth-century cleric and theological writer, hit the nail on the head in 'The Spirit of Love' when he wrote: 'Perpetual inspiration is as necessary to the life of goodness, holiness and happiness as perpetual respiration is necessary to animal life.'

We need inspiration to be well. However, we sadly live in a world where a lack of inspiration is seen as the norm, and just the way things are. One of the reasons I am so passionate about what I teach and share is because I want to live in a world where there is an abundance of inspiration. To that end, I aim to be both the cause of inspiration through showing up in my work when I can, as well as encouraging, supporting and celebrating others who show up with their inspiration in the world.

I agree with these words of Marianne Williamson, who reasons that we are all here to share our gifts and transform the world back to love: 'We weren't just randomly thrown onto a sea of rocks. We have a mission – to save the world through the power of love. The world needs healing desperately, like a bird with a broken wing. People know this, and millions have prayed. God heard us. He sent help. He sent you.'

I sincerely believe that you are literally the answer to some people's prayers.

Twelve Tools for Tackling Resistance

Now you are armed with your list of reasons why you deserve to overcome resistance, here are a dozen of the most powerful and successful practical ways of getting through it to show up powerfully and authentically in your work and life.

1. Acceptance

Resistance seems to be part of the software of being human. You are subject to it, but you are not a victim to it. The denial of resistance can itself be a form of resistance, so it's important simply to be aware and accept that resistance does operate within you. Being harsh on yourself for experiencing resistance simply reinforces it. You may believe that by railing against what you don't want, you will eventually become free of it. But, by judging it in this way, you may become stuck with it, rather than liberated from it. Be kind, accept the resistance in your life and then choose to move beyond it. You can always make new choices.

2. Have courage in the face of fear

Sometimes it takes courage to act in the face of fear and resistance. In every person's success story, you are likely to find someone who has made a courageous decision. Occasionally, even simple things take a lot of energy and courage. As writer Susan Jeffers suggests, feel the fear, or doubt, and do it anyway. Courage is required not just the once, but regularly. Ultimately, we know deeply that on the other side of every fear lies a freedom. Your courage and your other resources are greater than your resistance, but you have to activate them. The only way to dispel fear is to look it in the face and utilise your courage. Courage is not the absence of fear – it's your triumph over it, revealing to you what you're truly capable of and who you truly are.

3. Consistently take small steps

Purposes are lived a step at a time; dreams are built one action at a time; character is forged one act at a time. Often a baby step is all you need to take to overcome resistance. Your very life depends on continuous beginnings, yet sometimes the greatest challenge is just to get started. There is something deep within each of us that conspires for us to remain safe within our existing boundaries, and to stay the same. Yet in order to harvest the potential riches of our life, our best bet is often to place our trust in the act of beginning. This isn't always easy, but in order to live a truly creative life, we should be continually prepared to cast a critical look at where we might be stagnating or where new beginnings might be ripening for us. If, for example, you were to write 150 words a day for one year, in a year you would have written over 50,000 words, which could be your book completed. Likewise, if you found just one new client a week, you could build your business successfully over a year or two.

4. Act in anticipation of inspiration

Sometimes we might not initially feel inspired to do our work, but when we start doing it and get into our flow, we begin to feel inspired. Someone once asked the writer William Somerset Maugham whether he wrote when inspiration struck him or at a particular time each day, and his answer was very revealing. He said: 'I sit down to write at nine each morning and fortunately inspiration strikes me at about five minutes past nine each morning.' I believe he meant by this that he didn't always feel like writing, but he disciplined himself to sit down and write anyway, and in so doing he initiated the flow of inspiration. Inspiration has to find you working before it starts flowing for you.

5. Be good enough rather than perfect

We have touched on the problem of perfectionism in Chapter 4. If you have a perfectionist streak in your character, it is probably difficult for you to do anything that you believe isn't perfect. It's important to understand that even though something isn't perfect, it can still be very valuable. Train yourself to see value in what you *actually* do, rather than *plan* to do one day. By simply starting to act, however imperfectly, you can learn as you go and improve as you go, and get better and better. Tell yourself that you are not your actions alone, and that who you are is inherently valuable.

6. Trust in the process of your growth and evolution

Whilst you may fear moving forward, or going deeper into yourself and expressing your True Self, you can trust that there are greater forces at work which actively want you to step towards fulfilling your greatest potential. You are being *drawn* forward. You may have heard that in the Kabbalah, the Jewish mystical tradition, it is believed that every blade of grass is cared for by a presence that shouts 'grow, grow!' at it and which participates in its evolution. Imagine what presences could be encouraging your own growth! You are not alone, whether you believe in God, spirits, angels – or just in your own humanity. In 'Everything is Waiting for You', the poet David Whyte writes: 'Your greatest mistake is to act the drama / as if you were alone.'

7. Skilfulness, strategies, clear thinking and know-how

Your resistance may be fed by your fear of the unknown, your lack of knowledge or understanding. However, as you begin to know and understand, your fear subsides and your confidence increases. So, sometimes in order to overcome resistance you may just need to learn something, to train, to develop a new skill, understand a strategy and have a clear a plan of action. It may be that clear thinking alone gets you past your resistance. I am continuously amazed by how people in my seminars suddenly feel so motivated when they see how they could do something; where they once couldn't see a path, one emerges. Learning how to do things is a massive part of beating resistance and succeeding; most successful people are lifelong learners. As mentioned earlier, my only reservation is that sometimes 'learning more' can itself become a form of resistance. I've met some wonderful people who have become caught in the trap of being the perpetual student, and who do not fully act on what they already know. So I suggest you act on what you already know *and* learn more when you need and want to.

8. Get support and encouragement

There are times when you will need someone to believe in you and encourage you. There may be some thresholds you cannot cross alone, when you will need to be supported and cheered onwards. Daily portions of encouragement can be the fuel that keeps your hopes and dreams alive and well. You might need to find someone to believe in you, who can hold you to a higher vision than you hold yourself. Then you can grow into what that person sees in you.

9. Commit and make yourself accountable

You may find that you sometimes give yourself what I call 'excessive wiggle room': you say you'll do something but then you let yourself off the hook and don't do it, and there are no obvious consequences. By making yourself accountable to someone other than yourself, you will feel compelled to follow through and take action. Accountability could be the ingredient you need to start moving from wishful thinking to manifesting a new reality in your life. You can make yourself accountable to friends, colleagues, a coach, a minister or counsellor. Ultimately, of course, you will always need to remain accountable to yourself.

10. Focus on the rewards

When you are in resistance mode, your time scale will often shrink down to how you feel *right now*. It can be easy to lose sight of your long-term vision, including the blessings and possibilities that lie on the other side of your resistance. If times are tough, then focusing on the possible rewards – material, financial, creative, emotional or spiritual – can be what gets you through. You can motivate yourself by what you will achieve, receive or become.

11. Energy healing and clearing

I am of the opinion that much of our resistance isn't necessarily even 'ours' in that we can 'inherit' other people's resistance, whether it be from family, community or ancestors. So we are carrying what were originally other people's fears, doubts and resistances. I have participated in many energy healing and clearing sessions to remove those sorts of energies from my own field and have found them to be incredibly valuable.

12. Laughing at resistance!

It can be really helpful to treat resistance lightly. It can be heavy stuff, shameful and pain-inducing when we realise what we have been doing. To be able to smile genuinely and laugh at some of the crazy beliefs we have, the mad stories we tell ourselves and the crazy things we do to undermine ourselves, is a true leadership gift. We all do these crazy things. Finding humour can reduce the heaviness and be liberating.

Going Public and Sharing Your Work with the World

I lost count years ago of the number of times clients have told me about the book they've written that no one has got to read, or the songs that no one has heard, the feelings they haven't shared, the insights and wisdom no one has yet benefited from. It can seem the easiest option simply to keep such things to ourselves, which means that we don't risk any of the 'bad' stuff that we fear might follow if we put them out into the world. But, as we have seen, if we do this, we also rob ourselves, and the world, of our 'good stuff.'

There is always more finessing we can do. Every time I finish a book, I am ready to start all over again, now that I understand the territory better. I almost have to have the text prised out of my hands. But I have come to realise that by letting the current book go and putting it out in to the world, I am free to write the next one, rather than getting caught up in writing the one 'perfect' book.

Creativity is never really finished with us – we can simply make a choice to let go, share our work and live with what happens next. Letting go of attachment and sharing your work with the world is one of the most generous things you can as a human being.

Get a Few (Public) Failures Under Your Belt!

Most of us rightly fear some kind of public shame or humiliation, of not living up to our self-image. We don't want to be messy beginners; we want to emerge fully formed. However, I am a great fan of failing a few times, often publicly. Why? Because the idea of it terrifies most of us, and we will do anything to avoid it. Instead, we are easily tempted to edit and distort ourselves in order to be what we think will be acceptable to others. But the reality is that even if it does hurt as badly as we feared, once we have experienced it, we start to feel freer. The threat of failure no longer hangs over us like the sword of Damocles.

In 2002, I hired a 200-seater venue in London to give a talk on the subject of 'Spirituality and Success' soon after my second book, *Unconditional Success*, was published. Come the evening of the talk, six people arrived. It turned out that spiritual teacher Deepak Chopra was in town too that night, giving a talk on his book *The Seven Spiritual Laws of Success* to a sold-out 700-seater venue.

I lost money, I felt stupid – and I survived. It was one of the worst things I feared might happen to me, but once it happened, it actually felt quite liberating. I learned a lot from the episode and, most importantly, I was no longer so scared.

There is something very liberating about facing and surviving one of our greatest fears. Ultimately, our feelings are just experiences like any other. Obviously, some experiences are more pleasant than others, but when we have the confidence to know that we can survive and even thrive after seeming to 'fail', we become a lot freer.

Radical Trust

Radical trust means showing up with as little attachment to results as possible: you show up, put your work out there with a lot of hope, a lot of expectation, but no ability to influence people's reaction to it. That's trust.

We hope for success, adulation, validation, purchases. We fear criticism and being judged and criticised. The reality for most of us is that we are not going to attract the haters. We are going to be met with indifference. Nothing much will happen. We are probably not even going to make enough of a blip on most people's radars to warrant criticism. Yet still we hide ourselves away.

The Ultimate Act of Self-Sovereignty

Shipping our work to the world is an act of self-sovereignty, especially when we are acting on our own incentive, determined to get our work out there without any assurances about how the world will respond to it. It can be an on-going process and while there are no guarantees of success, it is better to venture than to refuse inspiration's invitation.

One client, Cara, had created a product but had not yet launched it publically. So we looked at her resistance, her reasons for overcoming it, and her practical baby steps going forward; and over six months of coaching, she launched her cards. She got tremendous feedback for them and new doors opened for her. Her confidence grew and her sense of power and possibility expanded.

What is it that we are *really* resisting when we refuse to act on our inspiration? What if, fear of failure aside, we are really resisting our power and our grandeur of spirit – and how amazing we are? What if we are resisting our ability to lead and show up in all our potential brilliance? We're going to be looking at this next.

PART THREE:

YOUR POWER TO SHOW UP

CHAPTER 7
Your Power to Show Up in Your Brilliance and Grandeur

'To accept that God has given each of us a magnificent role to play on Earth merely because we're human; that we were born with a perfect script etched on our hearts; that its not to our personal credit, but to His greater glory, that each of us is brilliant – such are the truths that set us free from the ego's lies. Mystical understanding is a ray of light, God's kiss that transforms us back into what we truly are. Each of us can put down the burden of our false self and allow our truth to emerge.'

Marianne Williamson,
The Age of Miracles – Embracing the New Midlife

Janey is a successful author, podcaster and trainer. She hired me to help her regroup and relight her fire after the painful breakdown of her relationship with her business partner.

At the beginning of one of our conversations, she told me, 'You asked me a great question in our last session, about who my ideal clients are. I've come to realise that my ideal coaching clients are the leaders of companies with a turnover of at least a billion dollars, and their leadership teams.'

No one had ever said that to me before! I tried my best to look cool, as if I always had conversations about the leaders of billion-dollar companies. Secretly, I was wondering whether she might not be being just a tad grandiose.

But as we talked more, I learned that in her previous career in a major plc, she had been responsible for a budget of over £1 billion across Europe. So she was simply describing the reality of her life and her work. From her own experience, she knew that these leaders are often surrounded by people who don't challenge them, and that they are shielded from some aspects of reality; and she knew she was providing a great service by going in and helping them see the truths that others tried to protect them from. She helped them apply critical thinking to ideas and strategies without being critical of the people offering them. It was a great skill and service to provide, one that not too many people were capable of delivering to leaders in this sphere. She wasn't intimidated by these people either, mostly men, and could meet them energetically at their level. She respected them, and they respected and valued her, her input and perspectives.

So I had been wrong. Janey wasn't being grandiose at all; she was talking about her grandeur, and our coaching was about how she could show up in her grandeur more consciously and consistently, rather than shrinking herself down and playing smaller than she truly was. This work represented her at her best, delivered to the people she knew she could most powerfully serve. This was her personal 'brand' and her positioning. (In Chapter 11, we will be exploring the concept of our Signature Work in more depth.)

The Other 'I'

Often, when we use the word 'I', we are referring to our ego, the self we associate with our personality. Yet this is not where our grandeur resides. Our grandeur exists in our 'other' Self, our True Self, which is often not the loudest voice in our mind. But it's there in us, and I think this is where inspiration resides too. This is the Self that came with our creation and which is not affected by the shenanigans of this world. Juan Ramón Jiménez described it in his poem 'I am not I' (translated by Robert Bly):

> I am not I.
>   I am this one
> walking beside me whom I do not see,
> whom at times I manage to visit,
> and whom at other times I forget;

> the one who remains silent when I talk,
> the one who forgives, sweet, when I hate,
> the one who takes a walk when I am indoors,
> the one who will remain standing when I die.

As spiritual beings, we are vast and mysterious.

The Ego's Clever Trick

One of cleverest tricks that the ego manages to pull off is to get us to believe there isn't any grandeur in us. Indeed, it has us believe that we are being grandiose even to think that we might possess grandeur. It is as if the ego manages to switch the labels in order to prevent us from knowing our own true nature.

Most of us go around believing we are inadequate, we aren't enough; perhaps even that we are evil, bad or sinful in some way. And when someone does own their grandeur, they are often attacked or criticised for being deluded. Of course, there are people who are deluded and who are on ego trips, which just compounds the challenge for us! Or we may turn these individuals into gurus and worship them, rather than see that they are simply holding up a mirror for us to our own true nature. A true guru is really a destroyer of ignorance, so great gurus help us dissolve our ignorance and reveal our own splendour to us.

When It's Grandiose to Be Humble

'There is a place in you where nothing is impossible. There is a place in you where the strength of God abides.'

A Course in Miracles

My friend James has been writing a book for around six years now, and is around two thirds of the way through it. He doesn't have a problem with the content, because his material is already being shared around the world as part of a programme taught by a spiritual organization that he belongs to. The issue is that his name doesn't appear on the course;

it is branded under the name of the spiritual organization. Personally, he is invisible in relation to it and there is no credit associated with him.

As we talked, it became clear that the idea of putting his name on the course book and 'owning' the material brought to the surface many of the messages he'd received from his childhood and family. He realised he carried beliefs such as: *don't be big-headed*, *don't think too highly of yourself*, *don't get too big for your boots*, *don't be proud of yourself*, *don't brag or show off* and *don't take personal credit for your achievements*. All these childhood messages were confusing and derailing him as an adult. Part of him obviously wanted to complete the book because one of his core values was to be of service; and he was consequently berating himself for not finishing it and being of service. He understandably wanted to remain humble and he was afraid of going an ego trip, being grandiose and then being judged and criticised.

So I encouraged James to acknowledge and then step into his grandeur by finishing his book as an act of generosity to himself and the potential readers around the planet.

There is a Grandeur in You, Right Now

'The most effective way of touching lives around you is to break your own barriers.'

Sadhguru, Indian yogi, mystic and author

One of the core beliefs that underpins my work and my thinking is that there is a grandeur that came with our creation. It is the essence of who we are, right now, and who we have always been. We can deny that grandeur, forget it or fight it, but that has no impact whatsoever on it. Our grandeur is indestructible. Our ego tries to play God by making us forget our true divine nature. Our true brilliance only emerges in the absence of self-judgement.

In the forgetting of our grandeur, the ego creeps in and says, 'Don't worry, I'll make up for your loss. I will inflate you so you feel significant and important, and that you matter.

I'll create another sense of identity for you so you don't have to feel like you are nothing and useless.' So the ego part of ourselves creates what I tend to think of as grandiosity. Grandiosity is your ego's attempt to offer you back the grandeur in you that you have forgotten. Yet all the while, your true splendour remains largely imprisoned within you.

Grandiosity won't Make Us Happy

Sadly, even significant leadership success might not make you truly happy if it is based in grandiosity rather than a grandeur of spirit.

When we first met in June 2018, Steven introduced himself to me by saying, 'For my fiftieth birthday last week, I hired a private jet to take me and some of my best friends to Moscow to see the World Cup final there, and then stay over and fly back the next day.'

He was the joint CEO of a successful publishing company, who had been chasing the idol of success for many years, and by most people's standards, he had arrived at it. But then he confided in me that it hadn't really delivered happiness to him.

So we started to explore the idea of what true happiness and success might really mean for him, and the 'already enough' principle that I touched upon in Chapter 3 – that we don't need to go looking externally for sources of happiness, but to connect with our True Selves.

From Seeking to Finding

One powerful shift we can make is to go from seeking to unwrapping. Ego is all about seeking; however, authentic leadership is about going deeper to unearth what already is within us now – unearthing our innate qualities, becoming curious about ourselves and unwrapping our capabilities. This is not self-indulgence, but about being genuinely curious with respect to the impact you can have, the inspiration you can offer, the positive influence you can be and the difference you can make.

Obviously, as we explored in Chapter 4, we are all up against resistance. Moreover, some of us don't believe in what we have to offer – that there truly is a lot in us left to unwrap.

Re-imagining Humility

A key question we can consider with respect to inspired leadership is this: what do we understand true humility to be?

When I was younger, my idea of humility was to play small, to think badly of myself and not to dare to think there could be anything good or of value in me. Like my author friend James, I believed I shouldn't brag or be too proud of myself. Essentially, I believed that true humility was about putting myself down. Others had light and gifts, but not me, so I shouldn't show off.

That didn't stop my inner impulse from wanting to share my light and my gifts, but I was so tough on myself that when I did that I would berate myself for days afterwards, as my conditioning had taught me that I should tone myself down and diminish myself; then I was being good and humble.

When I became a published author for the first time, I believed my book and the information in it were everything, and that I was nothing really. It's taken me a long time to believe that I am 'something' too, and that my ideas and information are not the best part of me. This kind of conditioning is a hard habit to break.

Disowned Grandeur

For years, I was judgemental about confident people who appeared to play a bigger game with their lives. I told myself that I couldn't and shouldn't try to be like them. I saw them as self-inflating and arrogant, but at the same time I was secretly envious. Yet for me the choice seemed like a dilemma – either shrink myself or inflate myself. Neither option seemed that attractive! Their grandeur was part of my shadow self (see Chapter 5).

Becoming a student of the spiritual text *A Course in Miracles* in 1995 helped me a lot, especially a few specific pages that talked about the difference between grandeur and grandiosity. The *Course* teaches that true humility means accepting and acknowledging your grandeur. Anything else, it says, is actually grandiose. It teaches that the reality of who we are, rather than who we think we are, is that we are a child of God. It is the only thing that we are actually 'victim' to, meaning that while we might try to hide or deny this, there is nothing we can do to change our true identity. It's major stuff.

The Two Forms of Grandiosity

'Ego-trips' are an obvious form of grandiosity, whereby we puff ourselves up and inflate our accomplishments. However, I think it is less obvious to many of us that putting ourselves down excessively and deflating ourselves is also a form of grandiosity.

I remember how challenging I found it when someone once said to me, 'Get off the cross and stop crucifying yourself. We need the wood!' But I came to understand that when we put ourselves down, we aren't able to be really present. Instead, we are holding ourselves back from life and from the people who would love us to be more present to them. Putting ourselves down is actually a form of self-indulgence, which gives many of us yet another opportunity to beat ourselves up!

Both aspects of grandiosity – inflation and deflation – are so commonplace that we often don't even recognise them. There are some clues in the timeworn scripts that we repeat about ourselves:

Deflation

- I don't matter.
- I have nothing to offer.
- I am inferior.
- I am not as good as….

- Nobody suffers in the way that I do.
- I am a hopeless loser and there is no future for me.
- Don't worry about me, as long as you are happy.....
- I've blown it and there is no way back.

Inflation

- Only I can do this.
- I need to be your saviour/rescuer.
- I am the best.
- I am superior and the righteous one.
- I am special.
- I am so much more talented/ informed/clever...
- I am the chosen one.
- My opinions are the only ones that count.

Recognise any of these? Once you become aware of these thought-patterns, you will find it much easier to tackle them.

Being Delivered to Your Own Brilliance

Spiritual teacher Marianne Williamson says: 'We often pray to God for a brilliant partner, job, career, business or boss. Actually, it is much more powerful to pray to be delivered to our own brilliance so that we can bring it to our partner, business, career or work.' This is an incredibly important idea.

It suggests that as well as the leadership skills that we are already manifesting in our work, there are probably more leadership gifts in us, just waiting to be unwrapped. We are innately resourceful and have only manifested a proportion of our talent and capabilities so far. So, let's pray for more brilliant and inspiring leaders in the world, and let's also pray to be delivered to our own inspiring leadership and gifts.

Many of us will have glimpses of our brilliance; in fact, part of our journey is about getting to know ourselves well, so we can understand the true nature of our soul and what we were created for. Then we can gradually build the spiritual musculature that allows us to live more from our strengths and to express these in the world.

Becoming an Inspired Thought Leader

Will hired me to help him look at where he might go next with his work and vocation. He'd had an Irish Catholic upbringing, and had been brought up not to show pride in his achievements. He had worked a lot in pastoral care in academic environments. His issue was that he was very bright and had completed a PhD, but not done as much as he might with the results of his research. His niche was 'Successful Academic Transitions' and a significant part of his work involved helping students to progress through the institution and the academic world, and to transition successfully into the world of work.

While, like many of us, he'd had a thorough training in humility, he kept being invited to speak at conferences, without even trying, and was frequently sought out by senior clergy and even politicians for his insights!

I asked him, 'What other opportunities do you think might exist beyond the university that you currently work in? Are you interested in showing up more and seeing if there are other opportunities for you out there?'

He accepted the challenge to see if he could initiate more opportunities for himself under his own steam. So he put out a few feelers and then found himself being invited to speak at even more conferences, interviewed on Vatican Radio, and then being offered jobs. He was also invited to a meeting with senior leaders of the Anglican Church. Yet I could tell that part of him wanted to dismiss these as random opportunities.

I challenged him by delivering what I have come to think of as 'a loving kick up the bum'! I said, 'Will, you are a thought leader. You are being sought out for your knowledge, experience, wisdom and insight. Do you see that?'

A small part of him did see it, yet he struggled to believe it. The invitation here was to evolve how he saw himself – from being an experienced practitioner who'd managed to complete a PhD, to a man who truly was capable and who wanted to have a bigger influence on global education.

Because he was so immersed in his field, he saw patterns and possibilities that other people didn't see. If he wanted to take it up, here was an opportunity to 'play a bigger game', not out of grandiosity but out of a place of personal grandeur, which was entirely consistent with, and indeed the fulfilment of, his theology.

Somewhat ironically, given his line of work, it was time for him to graduate into the next chapter of his life.

A Man in his Grandeur

'The grandiosity of the ego is its alternative to the grandeur of God. Which will you choose?'

A Course in Miracles

On 31 January 2014, I met the Archbishop Emeritus of Cape Town, Desmond Tutu. Five years earlier, my friend Howard Carter had introduced me to Mike Dickson, a lovely man. One of Mike's claims to fame was being the inspiration behind Whizz Kids, a mobility charity that has so far raised over £100 million. Mike then went on to found the Rainmaker Foundation, whose purpose is to make the world a better place for all, and I had become a Rainmaker, one of the organisation's members who shares its ambitions. Mike had managed to persuade Desmond Tutu to become the patron of the foundation.

This year, one hundred Rainmakers and others connected with the community were invited to an evening with Desmond Tutu – or, as he likes to be known, the Arch – at the Haymarket Hotel in London. I was excited; I have known about the man all my life but wondered what he would be like in the flesh, especially now he was eighty-four years old. I had read his book *God Has a Dream* and loved his messages.

Before he spoke that evening, we were invited to sit and chat with him. I thanked him for being who he is and doing what he does. The Arch was very gracious, and we talked for a moment about love and inspiration.

When he stood up to speak, I was shocked, but in a good way. For the first five minutes, I thought this man had actually *missed* his calling – he should have been a stand-up comedian! He was so funny, he had us all in stitches; partly, I expect, because we didn't expect him to be that entertaining, especially while wearing full clerical garb.

But what touched me most about my time with him?

He wasn't just a speaker, he was an orator – which means, in my eyes, that he *is* his message rather than that he has a message to impart. His grandeur of spirit shone through. I was inspired by his humour, graciousness and his genuine positivity, which had been born out of considerable personal suffering as well as from witnessing so much suffering. He had experienced so much prejudice, hatred and evil in his life, his country and around the world, yet he had come out speaking and teaching about how wonderful human beings are.

One of my favourite lines in *A Course in Miracles* is this: 'The holiest spot on earth is where an ancient hatred has become a present love.' To me, the Arch personified that hope of transformation, moving from fear, pain and hatred into understanding and ultimately love. He has taken a stand for love in the world rather than standing for condemnation, revenge and retribution. He *inspires* people to change rather than tries to force people to change through judgement. His light helped kindled millions. His stand for higher purpose leadership and love in the world continues to fuel my own desire to stand up for love too.

The final piece in the jigsaw didn't fall into place until a couple of months afterwards, when I met up with Mike again. Mike said, 'Have you seen the new book the Arch has written with his daughter Mpho? It's called *The Book of Forgiving*.' Suddenly it all made sense. That's why Desmond Tutu is able to be who he is: he actively practises and teaches forgiveness. The Arch is a living example of the power of forgiveness, a power that is available to all of us.

They say never meet your heroes, because you'll be disappointed – but I certainly wasn't. I think one of the deepest purposes of life is to rip off the mask from fear to reveal the love hidden behind. To that end, I would encourage you to cease to live as if you are small, and to claim your authentic magnificence.

Two Drivers of Leadership
It dawned on me that the Arch exhibited a different kind of leadership to what we are used to seeing. His leadership was narrative led rather than competition led. He wasn't saying that South Africans were better than anyone else, or that people of colour were better. He was telling a story, weaving a narrative and sharing a worldview: that 'human beings are basically good and contain divinity; they are God's hands and feet, together we can transform this world and make it a better place. People just learn to be bad and then do bad things.'

Whether it's articulated or not, all leadership is driven by one of two philosophies. Your leadership is either competition-driven or story-inspired. You are either looking to win at someone else's expense, or you are looking to win 'at life' and make things better for everyone you can.

Self-Improvement vs. Naturally You

Part of the excitement of following your inspiration is discovering what is 'naturally you'. I once had the opportunity to speak with Julia Cameron, author of *The Artist's Way* and many other books, musicals, stage plays and songs. She is one of the least 'show-off' people I have ever met, but that she is pretty prolific is not in question! So, out of curiosity, I asked: 'Do you see yourself as exceptionally gifted or simply an example of what we can all do if we unblock our creative energy and gifts?'

You can probably guess her answer. She explained that she didn't see herself as anyone special or particularly gifted, simply a woman who was very available to her own sense of inspiration and relatively free to express herself in the ways where inspiration nudged her. She had unblocked her creative energy and her prolific output was the natural consequence.

The more you commit to unblocking your leadership and creativity, the more in touch you will naturally become with your grandeur. But this usually involves being very in touch with and open about your humanity. With this in mind, the next chapter is going to look at the power of openness.

CHAPTER 8

YOUR POWER TO BE OPEN

'When we were children, we used to think that when we were grown-up we would no longer be vulnerable. But to grow up is to accept vulnerability. To be alive is to be vulnerable.'

Madeleine L'Engle, ***Walking on Water***

Many traditional notions of leadership are about avoiding showing up with honesty and openness, almost at all costs. Leadership becomes a professional role that people play, and as a result they often aim to leave their personality and weaknesses out of it. But the majority of us don't find that very inspiring. Instead, we are more likely to be inspired by appropriate openness.

Based on those I have met, I think the most successful people offering leadership today tend to be open and honest individuals. Natural openness is a very attractive quality. And probably the most important reason that openness matters in leadership is that it is one of the most effective ways of fostering trust. Without trust, you are going to have to resort to force, manipulation, rewards and coercion, which might lead to short-term compliance, but not long-term confidence in your actions.

The Consequences of Being Open

In my first conversation with Shilpa, I was pretty surprised when she told me that she had moved house after experiencing a very significant personal betrayal, which had snowballed into the entire community turning against her and her business partner taking over the school she had created.

The most amazing part was still to come. She continued: 'So I moved and I found a potential new school, as well as a board who could fund the development of my new school, now that I had a track record. When they asked why I'd moved, I fudged an answer that would sound plausible. I was worried that if I told them the truth, I would jeopardise my funding.

'But the board came back to me and asked, "Why did you *really* move?" They obviously didn't quite believe me. Something must have felt incongruent to them, because I obviously wasn't telling them the complete truth. They didn't know what the truth was, but something must have seemed "off" to them. I felt caught in a dilemma.

'I spoke with a good friend who knew about the situation, and they strongly urged me to tell the truth. I realised I had nothing to lose so I told the funders what had really happened, feeling that I had probably blown my chances of their support and funding. But after listening carefully, the funders felt relieved and said, "Yes, now it finally makes sense!" Eventually this led to a position of trust, and they did indeed go ahead with the funding of the new school'.

Shilpa concluded: 'I was blown away. This went against all my inherited thinking that in business, you should create a professional image and you shouldn't share the challenges that are really going on in your life. I realised that my honesty and openness had not jeopardised my funding, but had actually secured the very trust that ensured it. It was a big lesson for me, and caused me to rewire the way that I thought about myself and business.'

There is a universal message in Shilpa's story: it shows how being real can be so powerful. Today, there is a massive lack of trust in many areas of life and work that can only be bridged by genuine openness and humanness. Yet, like Shilpa, many of us fear that being open could severely jeopardise our professional credibility, when the reality may well be that it helps us access our inner strength.

Too often we feel we can't or shouldn't be open. We may fear our own openness, and believe we should keep everything completely private, afraid that sharing how things really are for us could be business suicide. And the reality is that sadly in some situations, it might be. So, we play the game instead. The result is a lot of superficiality and a general lack of trust. We become a little inauthentic, someone who isn't that transparent and who doesn't really tell the whole truth. This can feed people's general cynicism about us, with the result that we dilute our creative power.

A New Form of Professionalism

If we approach leadership and professionalism as a role to be played, we are in danger of leaving ourselves, our personality and our True Self largely out of our leadership. It becomes just a job to do, rather than showing up in our work with openness and honesty.

At the other end of the spectrum, it's not all about us. But there can be a place in the middle – where we are very much in touch with our humanity and able to be professional and lead professionally. It is important to choose how open we are, and with whom. We should not feel compelled to share every detail, but to find a balance that allows us to bring our True Self into our work.

How to Encourage Openness

I used to think that people 'should' be open. But as I have become more open myself, I have developed a much greater respect for people's defences. I can see they are often there for a reason and that we need to let our defences go a little at a time, when we feel safe. After all, it has taken me years to be open about some aspects of my life.

In 2017, only about twenty years too late, I got to participate in Prime Minister's Questions. The PM concerned was Sir John Major and I had a chance to speak to him at an evening hosted by The China Exchange in London, rather than in the House of Commons. He was reflecting on how much more difficult he thought being in politics was in 2017, compared to his time, what with the pressure of social media, so little time to reflect and think before having to make decisions. He painted a picture of politicians feeling more scared and out of their depth than ever.

I put up my hand and asked: 'How can we make it easier for politicians to be open, to acknowledge their own vulnerabilities and to be more honest about their own difficulties and challenges?'

He thought for a moment, then answered, 'I have no idea!'

Well, at least he was being honest! He talked about how politicians are still invested in hiding their weaknesses and vulnerabilities, believing that either the media or other politicians will then exploit this information for their own ends. When it comes to honest debate about the important issues that affect us, we clearly have a big challenge on our hands, and we can pray that some people at least are inspired to lead the way with greater openness.

Work Cultures Afraid of Openness

Tanya is a lawyer who loves the whole area of data protection, as she believes strongly that we should remain in charge of what others know about us. She explained that she wanted to make the whole subject 'cool', and she came across as an incredibly creative, open and inspiring individual. I was shocked when she described what was going on for her at work, as it became clear that she was being bullied by her boss and other senior people. She explained that she just wanted to do a good job; she wasn't interested in office politics, yet she was getting caught up in the political wrangling and power-play of her company. Some people didn't want her to shine, probably seeing her and her potential as a threat, even though she had little interest in being promoted to their positions. So she was being kept in her place. And because she was young and black, a couple of the senior members of staff seemed terrified that she might take them to a tribunal.

After a challenging year that drained her energy and lowered her moral, she eventually decided to leave and see if she could find work with a company that valued her. She was offered many jobs, and took one with a 30 per cent pay rise, where the company valued the insight, experience, leadership and passion that she could bring.

The major lesson for her, she explained, had been to realise that there was nothing wrong with her for being open. Her only contribution to the initial problem had been to plant herself in a culture that didn't really appreciate what she had to offer. She had learned to stop trying to fit in where she didn't seem to be wanted and to stop wasting her energy fighting battles. Instead, she would focus on working with people where she was valued, supported and encouraged to blossom – and celebrated when she did blossom, rather than being kept in her place.

Permission to Be Open and Vulnerable

Some of us simply don't believe it's OK to be open. Either we were told at some point in our lives, or we decided from bitter experience, that being open is a sign of personal weakness. Instead, we try to soldier on; we keep our problems to ourselves; we stay strong and don't let anyone in. Openness might feel like it presents a threat to our very survival. We believe we have to hide away our perceived weaknesses and not let anyone else see them, so we overcompensate by trying to be almost superhuman.

Being open can cause us to feel vulnerable, at least at first, and we often aren't that friendly towards our own vulnerability. One of my favourite thoughts about vulnerability is that it is usually a quality that we admire in others, seeing them as courageous, valuable and open; but when we consider our own vulnerability, we perceive it as an unattractive flaw that ought to be hidden away. We might admire other people's openness yet dislike or despise our own.

However, being vulnerable is a natural part of the human condition and one that we can't escape, so the real question is how we learn to handle it, and what kind of relationship do we have with it. Do you judge your vulnerability or do you have compassion for it?

The Gift of Hepatitis

I certainly grew up believing it wasn't safe to be vulnerable and for many years I was scared of my vulnerability. I didn't know quite how to handle it – until experience taught me a valuable lesson.

At the age of fifty-four, I contracted hepatitis while I was working abroad. The strangely wrapped 'gift' was that I hated how vulnerable I felt as a result. In fact, I felt ashamed of my vulnerability. I had to be hospitalised, I was weak, I was dependent on the nursing staff and on Helen, and I had to be taken care of.

I hated that this had happened to me and I thought there must be something wrong with me for feeling so vulnerable and exposed. I think I was still running some old idea that I had to be 'invulnerable', almost superhuman, and when I wasn't, I had somehow failed.

So the illness broke me open in painful but helpful ways. Time for another round of divine surgery in order to open myself up to loving myself, even when I felt very human, weak and dependent.

The Bravery of Being Open

We each have to navigate our own path of openness at our own pace, rather than feel we *have* to be open. It is important that we stay in charge of ourselves and what we may or may not choose to reveal, to whom and when.

The reality is that we don't know how our openness will land with people, or how we will feel as a result of opening up. It is inherently risky, yet also full of possibilities and potential. The writer and researcher Brené Brown talks about 'shame hangovers', where we open up but then feel shame the next day for having done it and attack ourselves.

Openness has the potential to polarise audiences, clients or funders. It could connect us more deeply with people, creating bonding and bridging the divide, or they may end up feeling alienated by our honesty and perceived oversharing; we simply don't know, so it's a matter of professional discretion and judgement. However, it always pays to be open with ourselves.

What Have I Been Hiding...

On 30 July, 2014, I was at Heathrow Terminal 1, waiting to board a flight to Zürich. I was very excited. The week before, I had received an email from a woman called Antoinette, writing from Switzerland. She told me, 'It's my husband Andreas's fiftieth birthday next week. He loves your work and your books, and I wondered if I could buy a couple of hours of your coaching for him as a gift, as he's been struggling a bit recently.' At the end of the email there was a PS, in which Antoinette added, 'If you happen to be free next week, would you like to be a surprise guest at his birthday dinner, and then stay and spend some time coaching him the next day?'

Well, I don't get many invitations like that! I was able to free up my schedule, so I spoke with Antoinette that evening and we agreed I would fly over. She transferred some money, and there I was – heading off on another amazing adventure.

But besides feeling excited, privileged and honoured, I was also feeling quite choked up, which didn't make sense in the circumstances. While I waited for my flight to be called, I got a coffee and asked myself why. Then I began to realise that this invitation coincided almost exactly to the day with the date on which I'd left my corporate career to start my own business twenty-five years earlier. As I sat and drank my coffee, I reflected on how difficult I have found my journey through life on many occasions: how inadequate I've felt, how desperate I've been, and how close I've been to giving up and giving in.

Twenty-five years earlier, I nearly didn't start my business. After I left my corporate career, instead of fanning that initial spark of inspiration into a flame, I fell into a deep hole of suicidal depression for nearly twelve months. I signed on to the dole and I didn't want to live at all. What changed things was a simple but powerful moment in which I decided to choose life, and committed to saying yes to the adventure of my own existence.

I realised I was proud of myself for still being here. I was proud of finding the courage to keep going. Even when things had become terribly difficult, I hadn't given up. Even when I'd felt useless and defeated, I hadn't given in. The result of this was that my life had opened up in so many amazing ways. Wonderful opportunities had come my way, and with them beautiful ways to serve and contribute to others.

I had often told myself that I wasn't committed enough, but I began to realise I had actually shown tremendous courage and commitment, frequently in the face of great personal suffering and challenges. Despite everything I had experienced, I had simply stayed in the game. Stayed alive. Stayed on my path. I had found the courage to unearth, feel and then heal the vast amounts of pain that I had buried, rather than continuing to repress them.

And here I was flying off to Switzerland to have another amazing adventure. I was choked up because I had inspired myself by simply keeping living and not completely giving up on myself or on the gift of life itself.

I had never written about that episode of my life before. In a way, it was guilty and shameful secret. So I started to write about it. I showed the article to my friend Beverley, a coach and journalist, who encouraged me to publish the story on my blog. Initially I was massively resistant to the idea as I was in effect saying to the public: 'You know this stuff I've been keeping hidden for twenty-five years and not wanted anyone else to know about? Well, here it is now.' Yet I did publish and was shocked to see that within a week, I received more comments on that story than anything I had ever shared before. My openness had obviously touched something more universal and connected me to more people more deeply than ever.

Inspired by the response, Beverley encouraged me to write more stories from my own life, and then I got into a flow and I found it hard to stop! Just over a year later, in December 2015, I published *Pivotal Moments: my stories of courage, inspiration and vulnerability*, which included fifty-seven of my own stories. Essentially, I was choosing to share moments of my own life that I had spent the last twenty-five years hiding! It had taken me that long to feel comfortable enough to be that open.

Publishing *Pivotal Moments* was itself a pivotal moment for me – and as a result I started a whole new chapter of feeling more comfortable in my own skin. I'd lifted a weight off myself. Writer and civil rights activist Maya Angelou once said, 'The greatest burden we carry is our untold stories', and it began to dawn on me that the more open I was, the less I had to hide – and the less defences I needed as a result. My openness generated more openness, both in myself and others. Once people read the book, they felt safe to be more honest and transparent with me, allowing me to engage more closely with them in turn.

I have become more of a fan of the word 'openness', which means acknowledging our fears, when we feel weak, when we feel like we are not coping , or when we are in pain and suffering. But we can also be open about our joys, our passions and inspirations. For me, openness can cover the whole spectrum of experience and the whole range of emotions that we feel. We can become more open about all of them, enriching our own lives and the lives of those around us.

Beware 'Manufactured' Openness

In Chapter 5, I talked about 'manufactured' uniqueness compared to natural uniqueness. I think the same idea can apply to openness. Openness can sometimes be exploited a little cynically in business and leadership, and seen as another 'tick in the box' along the lines of: 'OK, I need to be open, so let me share a hard luck story to make people empathise with me and trust me.' So I think we need to be alert to when openness is real and when it is more 'manufactured' in order to manipulate others in some way. Sometimes this isn't obvious and it's only by getting to know someone over a period of time that we can tell whether they are being genuinely open or not.

Vulnerability as a Gateway to Confidence

You may remember Janey from Chapter 7, who engaged me to coach her when her relationship with her business partner had imploded. When she came for coaching, she was feeling very vulnerable, which wasn't a familiar or comfortable state for her. As a consequence, she was a little in shock – she felt she had lost her way and some of her confidence.

Like we all do, she initially resisted her sense of vulnerability, explaining she 'didn't want to go there', until it began to dawn on her that she really had no choice. Her strategy of acting tough wasn't working anymore. When she found the courage to accept her vulnerability and to dive into her feelings of pain and shame, a new inner strength began to surface for her. We got clear on her messages, on her target audience, on who she was working for. She also began to see that she didn't have to rely on a business partner to support her work; she could stay in her own sovereignty rather than give her power away to a business partner. Part of her resistance and shadow life had meant she had been spending her energy supporting the very person who was 'supposed' to be supporting her.

After six months of work together, she had grown into a new place. A healing had occurred within her. In one of our final conversations, she said, 'It's OK to be me! I'm professional, and I can also bring my humour, my passion and my audacity to my work. I'm happy that the more I am myself, the more "my people" will feel that resonance, and those that aren't will be indifferent or repelled. I know I'm not for everyone. I want to find more of the people I know I'm right for.' Then a few weeks later, she went on to say, 'On

Sunday, I had a group and did the best day's work I've ever done. I blew them away. Feels great to be back on fire again!' She became more confident that a sorting process would naturally happen: as she showed up more authentically, connection naturally happens.

This, to me, represents a high level of maturity and self-awareness – to develop enough genuine confidence to know that you are not for everyone so that you no longer try to get everyone to like you. By embracing your vulnerability you are more likely to develop true confidence. Janey was now embracing the power of being who she truly was.

She was becoming more audacious and active on her own behalf, saying to possible clients, 'I can help with that!' and even, 'I would love to help you with that!' She wasn't being grandiose – she was simply speaking the truth. She knew how company boards worked, what the dynamics were, and what the leverage points were. She knew how to identify and solve problems. She concluded, 'The more open I am, the easier it becomes.'

Opening Ourselves to New Horizons

Through my work with others, and in my own life, I have experienced over and again that the places we don't want to go – the uncomfortable, scary and painful places we resist going to –are often the very doors through which we are being invited to pass in order to see the new horizons that are waiting for us on the other side.

I once had a coaching conversation with the CEO of a services company, who decided as a result that he was going to ask his 300 employees what they thought was inspiring or uninspiring about his leadership. I knew how scary this would be for him, yet how courageous it was too. He got a lot of feedback, which helped him see the good that he was doing as a leader, as well as how to be clearer about the unintended impact of his leadership and how he could modify his behaviour. I was in awe of his commitment to his growth as a leader.

Controlling vs. Confidence
One way in which we might try to compensate for a lack of confidence is to by being controlling. Controlling what people know about us, controlling our own emotions and controlling those people who can trigger our feelings of vulnerability. As we grow in confidence, we are able to handle more of our emotions and our vulnerability, and the less we need to try to control anyone else around us.

We All Feel Vulnerable at Times
In 2013, at Ealing Studios in West London, Liz Trubridge was preparing to start filming of series four of *Downton Abbey* a couple of days later. We'd arranged to record a conversation about her amazing leadership style which I was going to share on my blog.

When I asked Liz about the challenges of operating in a world where big and fragile egos are often quite prevalent, she answered this way:

> What I have learned over the years is this: anyone who is willing to put their creativity in a public domain has to be willing to be vulnerable, to be brave enough to say, 'This is who I am and this is how I would like to interpret this.' What will come with this is a degree of fragility and fear, and that can often manifest itself in an ego. I think as a producer I have to be a little bit of a psychologist, to hear and understand the fear behind the behaviour, and allow people to feel safe and valued.

Something about her words had a powerful impact on me; then three weeks later it dawned on me exactly what it was. Even at the age of fifty-seven, there was a part of me that was still waiting for the day when I didn't feel vulnerable any more, and in the meantime I continued to be tough on myself, often judging and punishing myself for being 'weak'.

But here was Liz, producer of an incredibly successful TV period drama, effectively saying that dealing with fear and vulnerability was part of her job description. She was working with some of the top people in the world in front of and behind the camera, and realised that all of them felt vulnerable at times. And she still felt vulnerable herself at times. Yet she didn't see that as a weakness, but something to be managed in order to create an environment in which people felt safe enough to give of their best. She led by acknowledging her own vulnerabilities so that other people would have permission to share theirs too.

Sometimes we need to go first, and lead with our own vulnerability and that gives a permission to everyone to relax a little.

Who was I to be so worried about my vulnerability, then? At that moment I realised: the problem wasn't just that I felt vulnerable, the real problem was the relationship I had with my vulnerability. I wasn't particularly kind to the vulnerable aspects of myself. I was tough on them, judging myself as weak and even useless for being so vulnerable. I had criticised myself for not being much of a man because I experienced a lot of fear and vulnerability. I had an antagonistic relationship with my own vulnerability. It was a bit of a shock to understand this at last – but also liberating. I needed to create a happier, healthier and friendlier relationship with my terror and vulnerability.

Some of the people may appear to be together, but Liz has developed that X-Ray vision to see beyond the words and behaviour to what is *not* being spoken about, and to what is really going in inside people. She senses, and trusts her feelings, and acts accordingly, with compassion and understanding, rather than override her senses.

That was the key realisation: what if you are being invited to show more compassion for your vulnerability, to be kinder and more compassionate to yourself when you feel weak and afraid? Not to keep saying to yourself: *What is wrong with me? Why aren't I over this yet?* At last, you might be ready to give up the search for that mythical day when you will no longer feel vulnerable – and to stop being unkind to yourself for not yet getting there.

Share the Personal and Touch the Universal

I first met Amie Lee in 2005, when she joined an entrepreneurial community I was running at the time. She had left her job as an accountant to follow her dream of creating a new Chinese restaurant where the food was additive free. Her restaurant, Naturally Chinese, had experienced many challenges and problems, but had gone on to achieve success and she was now leading a million-pound business.

I knew her beginnings in the UK had been relatively humble, but it wasn't until 2018 that I heard Amie share more of the details. She was speaking at 'The Story Party' in London, an event founded by Beverley Glick. Essentially, there is a theme to each event, and six to eight people tell a ten-minute personal story based on that theme.

I was nearly in tears as Amie described how her family had been forced to leave Vietnam during the war, and how she had been one of the 'Boat People' I had heard of while I was growing up, but knew relatively little about. A charity sponsored her family to travel to the UK and they arrived here not speaking English, with pretty much nothing other than the clothes on their backs and a few possessions. By sharing her personal journey, she touched all our hearts and inspired us. And by being very personal, she touched on something universal.

The more we hear each other's stories, the easier it is to detect the universal themes in them and to see how similar we all are – the details might vary but the underlying patterns are the same. When we think we alone are experiencing challenges, we can easily feel separate and ashamed; whereas realising that we aren't the only ones to suffer can help to break down some of the barriers that seem to isolate us. That's what being open in this way can do. It can open hearts, create connection, develop empathy and build trust. Too often we fear that our openness might break trust and fracture relationships, but when we actually do it, we build trust and cement relationships instead.

Why is Openness so Powerful?

When people feel deeply connected to us, they will pay attention to us, learn from us and, if it's relevant, they may even buy from us, all because they are inspired by us. They choose us because they feel connected to us. By being open and sharing our personal truths and stories, we tap into a common humanity:

- Story is a universal medium – stories are a great way to inspire as well as educate and make points.
- The more we share something very personal, the higher the likelihood that what we share will have a universal resonance and capture someone's attention; people respond positively to authentic emotional expression.
- We are all hiding away 'untold' stories – I think many of us have episodes of our lives that we feel embarrassed about, or are still punishing ourselves over; yet sharing those stories can free us up of our emotional burdens while helping others.
- People trust us more because they know us and our inner world better, not just the image they may have of us.
- Openness allows for a deeper engagement with 'our people', the people for whom our work and leadership will have resonance and meaning.

Your Power to become Increasingly Defenceless

We build defences around those parts of our lives where we feel, or have felt, hurt, scared or vulnerable. We use defences to try to stay safe. But what if your greatest security actually came from dismantling those defences, rather than building them higher? This might seem counter-intuitive and perhaps a little crazy until you recognise that there is a part of you, your True Self, which lies beyond the capacity for hurt.

What if radical openness were actually your best defense? Consider this statement from *A Course in Miracle*: 'In your defencelessness your safety lies.' What might that mean for you?

In this chapter we have looked at the power of openness to engage people, to build trust and create bonds with those we serve and care about. One of the most powerful and courageous things you can do is to recognise, and to be open about, your shadow self and those parts of you that you have disowned, so that is what we are going to look at next.

CHAPTER 9
YOUR POWER TO OWN YOUR SHADOW

'The hope for humanity is that we may retrieve our shadow from our neighbour.'

Carl Jung

Muriel contacted me for coaching just after my first book was published. She worked in financial services and was doing OK, but her work didn't light her up, so she wanted some help to discover what she might have been born to do. During our first coaching session, I asked her a series of questions, yet increasingly I felt like I was drawing a blank. I was beginning to worry, and wondered if I might have to give her the coaching fee back. Then I intuitively asked her, 'Was there anything you loved doing as a child?' Suddenly I sensed her energy begin to rise.

Muriel talked enthusiastically about how she had loved sewing and making blouses when she was a teenager. She loved fashion and said, 'I would often think about a design for something while I was at school, and then come home and cut out the fabric, get the sewing machine out, and create the garment within an hour or two.'

I felt we were on to something. 'So why did you stop?' I asked.

'My mum told me I was wasting my time, and that I could never make a career out of fashion. We had a massive argument and I just dropped it. I never made anything again.'

Now she was in her mid-forties and a mother herself, and had not done any sewing like that for thirty years. I was feeling brave, so I offered her a coaching goal: to get her sewing machine out, then to design and make a blouse by the next time we spoke. Hesitantly, she accepted the goal, but I had no idea whether she would follow through or go into resistance by finding lots of excuses.

When she rang me for our next session, I asked how it went. She explained, 'It was so emotional! I cried my eyes out as I started to sew. I realised how angry I still was with my mum, but I was hurting myself by remaining angry. It was like I was reconnecting with that fifteen-year-old in me who I'd neglected and ignored. But I felt so proud and energised when I finished it. I did it – and I am wearing the blouse now.'

This was the beginning of a whole new dimension in her life – creating blouses and getting involved with fashion. She went on to say, 'My kids have remarked how I'm better with them; and they like seeing me happier and more fulfilled.'

The last time I heard from Muriel, she had moved to the UK and had been invited to create a whole collection to show at one of her daughters' schools, and she was very excited about the prospect. Her re-owned creativity was bearing fruit, and she was blossoming and re-owning her power. She had accepted something about herself that she had rejected and disowned many years earlier – and it was paying off for her.

Midlife as a Time to Re-own Aspects of Yourself

I think we often spend the first half of our life creating a self-image – deciding who we are, what we are and what we are not. What we decide we are not, or what we don't think is acceptable about us, we relegate to our shadow. Then we put the self-image out into the world and aim to succeed through it. Often it works, at least for a while, until we feel an inner call to be more 'real' in some way. Sometimes it is not until midlife that we start the process of examining and sorting through our shadow so we can re-own what we disowned about ourselves. While we are free to do this work at any time, midlife often gifts us with a more urgent invitation to explore this aspect of ourselves.

This shadow self is different from the shadow life that we looked at in Chapter 5. When we live a shadow life, we are living a paler version of the life we might be capable of living. We might do this by working in field that is related to the things we are passionate about, but not following through on our dreams; for example, we might work backstage in a theatre when we'd actually love to perform on the stage. However, our shadow self contains those aspects of ourselves that we suppress in order to fit in.

In 2000, I attended a weekend for men run by the ManKind Project (MKP). One of the guiding principles of this weekend was that every man contains 'gold' – meaning gifts, radiance and other wonderful qualities. The course taught us that every man also contains shadow – disowned qualities. One of the goals of MKP is to help men find, honour and feature their gold, and to become aware of their shadow and integrate it, so they don't act it out unconsciously.

Too often we are tempted to blame someone or something else for the things that we don't like about our lives, such 'you made me do it', or even 'the devil made me do it'. But blaming others generally leaves us feeling powerless, because we are demanding that someone or something else change for us to feel different. Whether we are male or female, if we consciously take responsibility for both our gold and our shadow, we are on the path back to our power.

While sometimes it can initially be painful to reconnect with our gold – our lost or neglected dreams, as Muriel experienced when she rekindled her love of sewing – it can also be a poignant and energising experience, leading us in new and powerful directions. The Swiss psychologist Carl Jung wrote: 'The greatest burden a child must bear is the *unlived* life of the parents.' I don't say this so as to guilt trip you for one moment – just to encourage you to realise that your being happier and more fulfilled does not represent a selfish act on your part, but represents a real blessing to you and the people around you. The world needs more truly alive and inspired people.

Your Shadow also Contains the Best of You

You might think that your shadow self is formed exclusively of potentially harmful qualities such as anger, rage, vengeance, violence, dishonesty, lack of integrity, blame and greed, as just a few examples. In which case, the idea of exploring and facing your shadow probably isn't particularly inspiring. But one of the most inspiring and liberating notions is that your shadow contains many of the most beautiful and powerful qualities you possess, as we saw in Muriel's case. You are likely to have disowned so many of your positive qualities too. In this way, many of us have disowned our creativity, our leadership, our compassion, kindness, spirituality and our exuberance and vivacity. Wanting these aspects of yourself back is a powerful motivator for embarking upon shadow work.

So my approach is that your shadow also contains your gold. In fact, the Swiss psychologist Carl Jung described our shadow as 90 per cent pure gold. You can reclaim the pure gold that you have lost contact with, but which has never gone away. Gospel singer Candi Staton puts it nicely: 'Your God-given gift may go dormant, but it never goes away. You can still pick it up again and when you do, you come back to life.'

Two Ways in Which We Tend to Deal with our Shadow Qualities

The two 'mechanisms' most of us use to handle our shadow are:

1. denial;
2. projection.

Denial and projection work as a double act.

The easiest way to deal with our shadow qualities is to deny we even have them; for example: *I would never be selfish/arrogant/aggressive/unthinking/unfair. I am not like that*. End of story. *But those other people, they are the selfish/arrogant/aggressive/unthinking/unfair ones, not us.*

I have already mentioned the impact that *The Road Less Travelled* had on me in my twenties, and I was fortunate to host a book launch event for M. Scott Peck at Alternatives. As a psychotherapist, he described how most people go into therapy convinced they are the good ones, even 'the righteous victims', while their family, partner or boss is the 'bad one.' But if they hang in long enough, he said, they begin to understand the part they've played in the family or team dynamics. They might then begin to see and own their shadow qualities and enter a new phase of emotional maturity, rather than remaining the unwilling victim.

Until we start to recognise and own our shadow, the world can seem like a house of mirrors. One of the great disservices we do, as Jung described in his writings about this aspect of ourselves, is to project our shadow on to others. In fact, most of us have likely experienced other people 'defining' us by telling us who we are and what qualities we embody by projecting their shadows on to us.

Tempting as it can be to feel we are right and they are wrong, the reality is that we are all a little more nuanced; there is light and dark in all of us. Spiritual teacher Gary Reynard wrote in *Disappearance of the Universe*:

> The [Course in Miracles] wants people to understand what is in their unconscious – so they can get rid of it. Most people, especially nice, spiritual people, don't know about the murderous thought system that runs this universe, or the hatred that's underneath the surface of their mind. Nor do most of them want to know. Most people want everything to be hunky dory. You can't blame them for wanting peace, but real peace is found by undoing the ego, not covering it over.

There is a Light in You Greater than the Darkness

Every time we judge and relegate a quality to our shadow, we lose some of our power. In order to regain that power, we need to be willing to face the challenging aspects of our shadow selves. And we can do this by understanding there is a light within us that can dispel its darkness. By shining this light on the hidden aspects of ourselves, our shadow becomes less frightening.

By looking at what lies in our shadow self, we can reintegrate it and re-own it. That's why shadow work can be so impactful. Each time we are able to acknowledge an aspect of our shadow, we can become a little more whole, less afraid, and we reclaim an aspect of our personal power, our voice and self-respect. We feel a little more confident in ourselves and a little less defensive. Our life expands. We can offer more effective leadership and bring people together rather than be tempted to project our own hidden character traits on to them and judge them.

I wonder if many leaders seek positions of authority so they can be in charge and avoid their shadow selves, their feelings of weakness and vulnerability, of dependence and powerlessness. If so, it won't usually succeed for long.

Truly Inspiring Leadership Moves Us beyond the Need for Enemies

So much traditional leadership has been about, and still is about, uniting a section of society against a common enemy – whether that be Jews, Arabs, the EU, single mothers, men, infidels and unbelievers, lazy unemployed scroungers, criminals, greedy business leaders, drugs barons, Catholics or Protestants, the competition, or the other political party, etc. We each pick our 'enemy' of choice.

There are many flavours to the ways in which we demonise and scapegoat each other. But one belief is common: *if only we can get them to change or even eliminate them, things would be so much better for us all.* We might embark on some kind of crusade to get rid of those we perceive as a threat, in the misguided belief that then we can just experience the 'good' and be more at peace. We believe that if we can get rid of what seems to trigger our 'bad' feelings, we wouldn't have to deal with our own feelings.

Personally, I am much more inspired by leadership that sees us all as one human family, with many facets to this family. Everyone we perceive as 'other' simply reflects a part of ourselves. Yet, as most of us don't even like everyone in our own families, there is slim chance that we will like everyone else in the world, even though they have just as much right to exist as we do. So inspired leadership isn't about forcing ourselves to like people. It is about the work of inner transformation and even forgiveness, rather than blame. It is about owning and integrating qualities rather than projecting them on to others.

Shadow, Blame and Responsibility

'More than those who hate you, more than all your enemies, an undisciplined mind does greater harm. Your worst enemy cannot harm you as much as your own unguarded thoughts.'

The Buddha

We can easily blame other people for being the cause of our own suffering. Then, the reasoning goes that if they are the cause we must create distance from them, punish them or even try to eliminate them, in the belief that this might solve our problems. Our emphasis is on getting others to change rather than seeking to change ourselves.

When we can accept that we are all in pain, we recognise that there are two paths we can take. Firstly, the 'righteous' path of being a victim and blaming those we see as the source of our pain, becoming tough and even fundamentalist in our thinking. Or we can choose the path of doing the inner work to transform our own suffering. In many ways, this is tougher because it is the path of taking responsibility for our problems, which is precisely what most people don't want to do. Yet the most inspiring leaders are often precisely those who do take responsibility for themselves, their feelings and experiences, and who invite others to do the same.

Inspired Leadership beyond Good Guys and Bad Guys

There is a tendency for most of us to meet others with judgement and criticism rather than compassion, kindness and understanding. In fact, there is a strand of leadership today which appears to define itself by its perceived enemies.

Such leadership is based on judgement and punishment, whereas truly inspired leadership is about helping people transform and correct their perceptions if necessary, rather than punishing them for how they have behaved.

Judgement never really draws the best out of others; only love and encouragement can do that. Yet the reality is that most of us make hundreds, if not thousands, of judgements about the people around us. Sometimes we voice these judgements out loud; more frequently we do our best to hide, bury and deny them, which is when they fester in our shadow selves.

There is a certain strength that comes from exerting our ego, from toughening up. And then there is a greater strength that comes from opening up, through the process of dismantling and dissolving our egoistic structures, and acknowledging our shadow selves. This has certainly been my own journey – from toughening up to opening up.

The Power of Meeting My own Shadow

While it can be relatively easy to define the shadow aspects of society through how it demonises other people or groups, the real power lies in looking at the shadow in our own lives and leadership. How does shadow apply to us personally?

I remember speaking with Sheldrick, a fellow co-presenter on a course at the University of Cape Town. He said to me, 'I found it easier to be liberated from the tyranny of apartheid than to liberate myself from my own inner tyranny!' It can sometimes seem easier to change the outer circumstances of our lives rather than transform the thinking that caused those circumstances. Well, it certainly has felt like that for me.

As I mentioned earlier, half a lifetime ago, at the age of thirty-one and after three years of soul searching, I eventually resigned from my corporate career. I wanted to change the circumstances of my life, believing that would make me happier. I wanted to serve others and I wanted more meaning in my life. The plan was that, after a mini-sabbatical, I would start my own business as a speaker, coach and event organiser, and maybe become a writer too. No one in my family had ever followed their entrepreneurial or creative calling to start their own business, so I didn't have a roadmap, but that was part of the adventure. I had been quite driven to succeed in my career and had done OK, and I had some faith that I could translate the ability to push myself into success in my own business.

So in April 1989, I gave notice to quit my job and then I rented my flat out for three months, which allowed me to travel to USA, New Zealand, Australia, Singapore and Thailand. I fell in love with a Canadian woman when I was in San Francisco, had a whirlwind romance with her in Australia, London and Toronto; then I organised a conference in London, and then, when it was all over, it was time to start my own business.

But instead of starting my own business in a blaze of excitement and inspiration, I fell into a black hole of depression and self-loathing as I mentioned on page 108. To be honest, I just wanted to give up and die. Cue my shadow – cue my own ferocious inner critic, which wanted me to believe I was a useless heap of crap!

During the course of my life, I had put a lid on so many thoughts, feelings and desires, and now that lid came flying off. All the 'stuff' I had been running away from seemed to have suddenly caught up with me. I had tried to outperform my inner critic and prove it wrong. Much that I had repressed and denied about myself suddenly seemed to be staring me in the face, and everything I had tried to bury was now saying, 'Here I am! You didn't get rid of me after all!'

I hadn't been kind to my sense of suffering; I had tried to bury it away and deny it, and to focus instead on being of service in business and relationships. I had felt ashamed of my own suffering, and I had kept busy to avoiding looking inside myself, afraid of what I would find; yet now here it was, in my face. My inner critic seemed to be claiming victory.

I realised I was going to need a bigger heart. I was being invited to expand the amount of compassion I felt for myself and for what I had experienced. I wanted to be able to love the 'failure' side of me as well as the 'success' side of me. At that time, I could hardly see any good in me, although I could see a lot of flaws.

When we encounter our shadow, there is often an emotional release involved. Buried and stored emotions will come to the surface to be released. This is not a pleasant experience, but through letting go of those emotions, healing and a new sense of freedom will follow.

With little structure in my life and a lot of time on my hands, my demons were having a field day. Suddenly I was faced with the shadow side of my drive to succeed. Deep down, I really felt like a hopeless loser. Through striving for success, I had tried to distract myself from all my painful thoughts and feelings, and it had worked for a while. But now my strategies of denial and repression weren't working so well any more. It was time for some divine surgery.

Besides experiencing the buried pain, and how tough I was being on myself, had started to explore my 'golden' shadows of inspiration, creativity, humour and comedy, and even of joy. I started to recover the healthy and natural child in me that I felt I had lost when I was young. My family had some dysfunction in it, for sure, and as a consequence I'd felt like I had needed to grow up too soon.

Painful as it was, luckily I also had enough support and awareness to gain an understanding of the process of transformation I was beginning to undergo. I did resist it a lot, but I also began the process of integrating my shadow. Gradually the lights started to come back on. Three decades later, the process continues, and it probably will for the rest of my life.

Even today I find that with too much time on my hands and not enough structure in my life, I can sometimes find myself 'behind enemy lines'. But I now know that the 'villain' is my own inner critic, which still likes to take any opportunity it can to offer me a running commentary on how badly I'm doing and how I should be doing better by now.

Three Ways of Looking at Your Shadow

I have now come to think that there are three main ways of approaching of self-transformation when we find ourselves in the position of not being happy with our lives, and not loving ourselves.

1. You are broken

In this model, we believe we are broken or sick in some way, and that we have a condition of some sort that needs labelling, followed by treatment with therapy, drugs or a programme of self-improvement. The hope is that once we have identified the cause, we can move from being ill to treating our problems and becoming well. There are certainly cases where some of us might benefit from professional medical or therapeutic help, and there is no shame in asking for this when we need it. However, in many instances, these sorts of belief are based on misguided judgements about ourselves being inherently flawed in some way. We think that we are broken and need 'fixing', so we go on a hunt for external 'cures' to make us feel better about ourselves.

2. You are bad

This model is about good and evil. We believe we are unhappy and suffering because we have done something wrong; we have sinned, or committed some crime against God or broken sacred rules or commandments. In some versions, we believe we are born sinful and have no control over this: we need to repent and be punished, or punish ourselves, and then we'll be pardoned or released, and can function more normally. Or we might think we have accumulated a lot of karma, for which we need to atone. Once we have suffered and been punished enough, we will be let off the hook and we will be happier. We believe we need accept our sinfulness so that we can be redeemed or saved.

3. There is Nothing Wrong with You, Just with Your Thinking about You

This model is based on the realisation that we have simply fallen asleep to, and temporarily forgotten, our pre-existing, greater True Self. You are still a precious child of God. What ails you has nothing to do with your being broken or being wrong or sinful. What ails you are the beliefs you hold about yourself, and forgetting who you really are. You are powerful and creative and full of gifts, but you may not be fully expressing those gifts and your love in the world. In this model, the remedy is simply to correct your fearful and judgemental thinking about yourself and to remember your essential Self. Your path is one of remembering your spirituality and true identity. This is the approach of *A Course in Miracles*, which teaches us to forgive and let go of the guilty and sinful image of yourself that you've created. This is not a path of self-improvement, because it is your thinking that is the problem, which got you where you are. It is a path of surrender and relinquishment, remembering that you have the love of God within you right now, and that incredible gifts reside in you right now, and you can show up and share them with the world. I have given this the label of Inspired Leadership, being led by the voice of love rather than the voice of fear.

We Over-Compensate for Our Shadow

When we have shadow beliefs about ourselves, we often act in the exact opposite way; for example, I had created a self-image of appearing to be very successful to mask what a failure I actually thought myself to be. When we believe we are essentially bad, we create and invent a persona that is good and righteous to replace this horrible image of ourselves – we create a compensation. Being the second child, I believed my older sister perceived me as a threat to her place in the family. So, I carried a belief within me that I was a threat. I overcompensated by burying this feeling, and tried to be as pleasing and accommodating as possible and never to be a threat to anyone. Yuk! The effort nearly killed me. But then that shadow would leak out and I would sometimes get angry and aggressive, even really threatening. And then I would feel so terribly ashamed. It was a cycle I went through for years.

Self-concepts are how we think of ourselves and how we see ourselves. They form significant parts of our identity. Depending on what we have come to believe about ourselves, we may work hard to 'prove' we are not as bad as deep down as we really think we are. For example, if we fear we are bad or evil, we work hard to be good; we fear we are lazy, so we work hard to prove how industrious we are; when we fear we are a curse on others, we try hard to be a blessing; we fear we are stupid so we strive to get as many qualifications as we can to prove how intelligent we are; if we feel we represent a threat, we may go out of our way to be accommodating. We can either compensate or even overcompensate for what we fear we are or believe we are. We can even believe it is grandiose to think there is anything good or positive about us. Yet, as we explored in Chapter 7, there is a grandeur in us which is part of our true identity, although relatively few of us live from that place of grandeur, even though it is blessing to others when we do so.

The problem with compensations is that all the rewards go to the role, not really to us. Ultimately, however well you play a role, it will be not as fulfilling as being yourself and accessing your truest qualities.

What are the Benefits of Meeting Your Shadow?

In many ways, the idea of meeting your shadow is not an easy sell. If someone were to say, 'OK, here is the deal – face your fear, face your pain, see all the gifts you have disowned and thrown away, acknowledge how much you have hated yourself and even abused and betrayed yourself. See clearly how little you have valued yourself. And then you'll have a happy ending!' Why on earth would you want to do that? What are the upsides of going through all that? Where does it lead?

In my experience, it leads to self-love and getting our true power back; it leads to feeling real and authentic, more at peace with yourself, and less defensive. Less energy has to go into defending your self-image and can instead simply go into 'being you'.

So where am I now after facing my own shadow? Well, I like and love myself much more than I used to. I am less critical of myself, and I am more of a champion for myself and my work. I can see my own significance more clearly, and the positive contribution I have made to people's lives. I feel more secure in myself. I have recovered many of my creative and leadership gifts. I feel more powerful. I feel more whole, more confident, and happier simply to be me, without feeling like I need to play roles to earn approval. I can serve other people better than I used to be able to. I don't feel as much of the despair I used to feel. I live my life in a sense of flow more of the time. I have more fun and more friends. There is a lot more meaning in my life.

Today, essentially, I feel more whole. I feel more unified. I feel less at war with myself and that more parts of me are headed in the same direction than there were before. I am no longer 'against myself' in ways that I had been previously. I am way off being any kind of finished article – but I like who I am, and that is precious to me.

What for me had felt like – and some people might call – a breakdown was actually the beginning of the process of breakthrough. Whilst I needed to attend to my pain and suffering, I also began to recover and re-own my power, my creativity, my confidence, my leadership and my disowned qualities – my shadow. And it's a journey that will continue for the rest of my life.

Moving Beyond Being at War with Yourself

One perspective that certainly has resonance for me is that when we go to war, we are really only fighting our own shadow; and, similarly, when we have power struggles with the people in our lives, we are resisting an aspect of our Self. By its very definition, our shadow is what we have judged to be unacceptable and which we try to punish or even eliminate in ourselves and in the world – even declaring war on it.

I am with the Russian writer Alexander Solzenitsyn when he wrote: 'If only it were all so simple! If only there were evil people somewhere insidiously committing evil deeds, and it were only necessary to separate them from the rest of us and destroy them. But the line dividing good and evil cuts through the heart of every human being. And who would destroy a piece of their own heart.'

It seems much easier in many ways to adopt a stance of 'moral superiority' and say, *I would never do that, I would never be like that, I'm superior!* Initially, it can take a lot of humility to work on integrating your shadow to restore your sense of power, rather than putting yourself down and beating yourself up even more. It's big stuff, though – because it means that when we are looking around at the world, and seeing all the things we hate, judge and dislike, we are really only looking at aspects of ourselves we don't like.

Leadership Means Recognising People Project on to Us, as We Do on to Them

When you do choose to become visible in your leadership, people are likely to project a lot of stuff on to you. This is why I believe cleaning up your act in terms of owning your shadow self is one of the most important aspects of leadership. It is quite possible to get lost in a world of projections. You project on to other people, and they project on to you. Figuring out who is 'right' and sorting through what's 'real' requires real discernment and emotional maturity.

Leadership is about being able to embody increasingly healthy and functional relationships. The old models of leadership are about leaders having all the power and being able to command a degree of compliance from their people. Leadership then is essentially about inequality. Today, modern leadership is much more about equality, and learning to relate well to others, both with people like us and those different to us – and great leaders are great relaters. They value difference and learn how to bring differences together. They are unifiers rather than projectors.

A Heart that Holds It All

'Though the human body is born complete in one moment, the human heart is never completely born. It is birthed in every experience of your life. Everything that happens has the potential to deepen you. It brings birth to new territories of your heart.'

John O'Donohue, Anam Cara

I know what it feels like to feel suicidal and worthless, abused and devastated; and I hope I now have empathy for others who feel similarly. I know what it feels like to be inspired, creative, powerful – and to know that I matter and play a part in enhancing people's lives; and I hope I can empathise with others who are seeking their own happiness too.

Today, I have developed a concept that I call 'a heart that holds it all' – all the experiences, painful and joyful, that I have known in the course of my life. I know which experiences I prefer, but I have compassion for everything that is involved in being human. The human experience can be wonderful and it can be horrible. It's often not an easy gig! It all just *is*, and these days I do my best to resist it as little as possible without judgement.

Shadow work can be the doorway to the next chapter of your success; as Elizabeth Lesser, the founder of the Omega Institute in New York, puts it: 'It was only through turning and facing my shadow that I was able to break open into a more genuine and generous life.' Often when we feel stuck in our life or leadership, this is an indication there is something in our shadow that we need to face and integrate.

A Willingness for Non-Resistance

'Whatever you resist you become. If you resist anger, you are always angry. If you resist sadness, you are always sad. If you resist

suffering, you are always suffering. If you resist confusion, you are always confused. We think that we resist certain states because they are there, but actually they are there because we resist them.'

Adyashanti

We may believe that either by burying our shadow, or projecting our shadow qualities on to others, we are saving ourselves from having to experience particular feelings. But through our resistance to our shadow, we may actually be causing ourselves even greater suffering, as the quote, above, from the spiritual teacher Adyashanti suggests.

It is not actually our shadow that causes us pain; it is our resistance to our shadow that causes pain. My experience is that we are often called to undergo a time of 'conscious suffering' when we allow ourselves to feel the feelings we have buried away. Poet Robert Bly calls these the 'ashes' times, when we go downwards rather than upwards in order to emerge finally and fly high. These are often times of great vulnerability and great humility. But out of that conscious suffering emerges a new birth, a new strength, a new self-love. Your heart is broken open to yourself and to others.

Why Do We Need to Look at Our Shadow to be an Inspiring Leader?

There are really only two modes of operation as human beings and as leaders: we can act out of love or out of fear, which also translates as operating from either understanding or judgement, inspiration or control, compassion or condemnation, forgiveness or grievances. Both paths lead to consequences.

We tend to admire those leaders who do their best to operate from inspiration, understanding and compassion. We admire the leadership embodied by the likes of Nelson Mandela, because these sorts of leaders choose not to give in to their ego's demands to judge, condemn and demand retribution from those who have done them harm. That's what we tend to find inspiring – men and women who are able to access a deeper part of them, their essence, soul or spirit, and to lead from place. Indeed, it is by looking at and integrating our own shadows that we can become inspiring leaders. We become authentic, we become whole – bridging the gap between our True Selves and the way we are in the world.

The Gap between Aspiration and Reality

So much great comedy and satire, and sadly tragedy, is to be found gap between who we aspire to be and how we want to be seen, and who we actually are. In Britain, we love sitcom characters such as John Cleese as Basil Fawlty in *Fawlty Towers* and Patricia Routledge as Hyacinth Bucket in *Keeping Up Appearances*, because their 'shadow' qualities of superiority and pomposity are continually being challenged.

Being blind to, or unwilling to acknowledge, our shadow is what trips us up. Although we might insist we have one set of characteristics, others can often see through our front straightaway. Whatever we insist we are, we probably also contain the opposite qualities. Whatever we take a stand for, we probably also contain the opposite perspective. That's why leadership can also be so challenging. To be truly effective we need to be constantly vigilant of our shadow, which in turn will make us less judgemental and more effective.

That's why your commitment to your inner growth can be so powerful in leadership: not to be right, but to be open and curious.

Owning and integrating your shadow – both its challenging traits and its hidden talents – will help you to regain your power and self-esteem. Ultimately, it will enable you to become more of the person you always sensed in your heart you could be, but had been afraid to live out so far.

In the final part of the book, we are going to look at how to embody inspirational leadership. Let's begin by looking at how to show up powerfully and clearly for the people you are here to serve, thereby making it easier for them to recognise you and your leadership.

PART FOUR:

YOUR POWER TO LEAD

CHAPTER 10
Your Power to Create your Signature Work and Unique Brand of Leadership

'Are you selling or are you showing up in the best light for the people who need you? Sales can be a service. And vice versa.'
Bernadette Jiwa, business philosopher, storyteller and author

Patrick had always been employed teaching students with special needs and he was brilliant at what he did. He was also a master storyteller and used stories to connect with children and help them learn in non-traditional ways. When the school where he was working closed down, he was made redundant. He kept applying for jobs and kept not getting them. As we spoke, I couldn't help but feel that he didn't really want the jobs, and that people were picking up on that. When I asked him whether he really wanted the work, he replied, 'Not really, but I'm afraid of money running out.'

In my experience, very few of us were encouraged to know and show up with what we love, in our power and brilliance, while we were growing up. We are more likely to have been brought up to think about how best to fit in and make ourselves employable.

I asked Patrick what he would really love to be doing at this point in his life. His answer was illuminating: 'I don't really want a job. I want to have my own business. I want to create a curriculum to teach teachers what I've learned about how using stories with children who have special learning needs, to help them achieve breakthroughs in their thinking and their behaviour.' He wanted to become more of an inspired thought leader, rather than the very accomplished practitioner he had been. It was time for him to evolve and create what I call our Signature Work.

We worked together on designing the curriculum for his new Signature Work. I could sense his inspiration returning as he thought about the wisdom he had accumulated which he would now love to share, and the impact he could have. And I could also hear the voices of resistance and his fierce inner critic, which were awakened: *Who are you to think you know more than everyone else? You've never run a business before, nobody would want to hire you. You're never going to make any money, so just go back to what you were doing before...* I expect you can recognise those voices too. Patrick was at the threshold of a whole new chapter: doing what he would love to do, rather than being employed; starting his own business; consciously offering leadership. It was no surprise to me that his resistance was kicking in, big time.

But he nevertheless dedicated himself to spending some time each day to draw up the curriculum and create his Signature Work.

Even Brilliance isn't a Guarantee of Success

Many people are brilliant at what they do, but even brilliance isn't a guarantee of success. I don't say this to dishearten you, but to help you identify the next steps.

Brilliance alone isn't enough: you need to identify clearly who your brilliance is for, how you can best serve your people, and how you can package your brilliance powerfully and clearly, so that people see what you offer as a solution to their problems. You need to be – and be seen as – trustworthy and capable. You will also benefit from developing your Signature Work around your unique style of leadership. Being brilliant is just the beginning.

Identifying and Developing Your Signature Work

It's very useful to understand the concept of Signature Work wherever you are on your leadership journey. However, the longer you have been practising and the more experience you have, in all likelihood the easier it will be for you to identify your Signature Work. Your Signature Work often follows on naturally when you've experienced a degree of experience and success, and been around the block a few times. Then you can spot the underlying patterns that continually show themselves in your area of expertise and develop a programme to address those patterns. Your Signature Work grows out of your expanding awareness.

You develop your Signature Work to help your Signature Clients – the two elements go hand in hand. However, you don't need to go on an external search to find out what it is; instead, I would invite you to believe that, within you, some part of you already knows what your Signature Work is and has a name for it. Like Patrick, your job is simply to allow this to surface into your conscious mind.

You may well develop your Signature Work by starting with your ideal client or clients in mind: in this case, you will need to know who you want to work with, and to understand their aspirations and struggles so that you can develop your Signature Work for *them.* In fact, today all you need to create a successful business are some Signature Clients. These are people you would love to work with and for whom you can offer the most value. Your Signature Work is the answer to your Signature Client's prayers.

Take a moment now to identify who your Signature Work is for: who are the clients you most love working with and can offer the best results for?

What is Your Signature Work?

Chefs have their signature dishes, sports people have signature moves, and musicians have their signature riffs or sounds for which they are best known. (My signature book remains *The Work We Were Born to Do*, even though I've written many others.) Signature means 'unique to you, uniquely expressed by you'. Your Signature Work, then, is you at your best – distilled, packaged and delivered to the world as something you will love to do which is also of service to others. In your Signature Work, your spirituality, gifts, experience and capabilities are brought together and delivered to the world.

Quite simply, your Signature Work represents you at your best, your most inspired and inspiring, doing your best and most competent work, and offering your personal brilliance, infused with your own spiritual DNA. It is you at your most shining and alive. It is what you were born to do, your calling, packaged authentically and delivered inspiringly and professionally to the world.

Your Signature Work clearly answers the following two questions:

- Who are you for? Who do you most powerfully serve? Who are your ideal clients and what problems and aspirations do they have that you have expertise in?
- What are you for? Where do you help your clients get to? What transformation do you help facilitate? Where are they when you start working together? Where are they likely to be when you have completed your work together?

These are questions that you will initially want to explore and answer for yourself, and then, as you become clearer, you will be able to communicate this information to attract your ideal clients.

Establishing your Signature Work is not arrogant; it is simply about knowing yourself clearly. It is about you in your grandeur, as we explored earlier. It is based on self-knowledge and self-esteem. It is about actualising your dream, and it serves as a contribution to the lives of others.

Why is Your Signature Work Important?

One of the most important things your Signature Work does for you is to answer the question: 'What should you hire me for?' As we develop clearer answers to that question, we become more hireable and people can advocate for us and recommend us more easily. Without a Signature Work of some description, we are less likely to be hired.

Our Signature Work demonstrates our authority, maybe even our thought leadership and expertise. Without a Signature Work, we might be well known and visible but still not generating much income.

Your Signature Work evolves your sense of identity as it can move you from being a 'commodity' to owning your 'artistry'.

Signature Work Gets Clients from Island A to Island B

In many respects, clients don't pay us for our expertise or skill. They pay us to support them as they attempt to achieve their own dreams, to reach their own promised land. We are there in service of their dream. Our Signature Work is therefore an act of humility and service, not about how great we are.

Marketing guru Tad Hargrave puts it eloquently. He describes people who take an interest in us and our work as being on 'Island A'. Our job is to understand 'Island A' and its needs, perhaps because we have spent some time there ourselves. Examples of Island A can include feeling overwhelmed, being overweight, feeling powerless, being uninspired or uninspiring, business failure, being broke, having low self-worth or being addicted in some way. There are countless Island As! However, this is emotional terrain that we are familiar with. For me, Island A means knowing what it's like to feel stuck in a successful corporate career, playing out roles, and not really being myself, while feeling that I had a calling in my heart that was aching to be fulfilled.

On to Island B: Island B is where others want to be and where we have the skills to take them. I now run a successful business and am living out my true calling. I feel I am being much more authentically myself. I know that journey never finishes, and I enjoy helping others embark on this adventure too.

As for the distance between Island A and Island B: in order to cross between A and B we have to understand our fear and resistance, and get past these. In my own case, I have needed to learn about becoming a leader, how to package and market my skills and expertise, overcome self-doubt and lack of self-worth. Some people call this our 'Signature System'.

Why Does your Signature Work Matter?

Our Signature Work puts us firmly in the driving seat. Rather than wondering 'what might I get hired for?' it's about stating, 'this is what I am gifted at doing, this is what I love to do and my Signature Work is what I want to be hired for.' When you can honestly and confidently say, 'I can help with that!' you know you are delivering your Signature Work. It is what you love to do and it is what you know people should hire you for, because you will get to deliver your best.

With less clarity around your Signature Work, you are less likely to be hired simply because people won't 'get' you and can't easily recommend you.

When you think of many leading names, actually you often think of their Signature Work. In my area, this includes books by the following:

- *The Artist's Way* by Julia Cameron,
- *Feel the Fear and Do It Anyway* by Susan Jeffers,
- *Men are From Mars, Women are From Venus* by John Gray,
- *Awaken the Giant Within* by Anthony Robbins,
- *How To Win Friends and Influence People* by Dale Carnegie,
- *Conversations With God* by Neale Donald Walsh,
- *A Return to Love* by Marianne Williamson,
- *The Power of Now* by Eckhart Tolle,
- *The 7 Habits of Highly Effective People* by Stephen Covey,
- *Become a Key Person of Influence* by Daniel Priestley,
- *The Hero's Journey* by Joseph Campbell,
- *Millionaire Messenger* by Brendon Burchard
- *Making A Living Without A Job* by Barbara Winter
- *The Journey* by Brandon Bays
- *Loving What Is* by Byron Katie

These people are known for their work as well as for themselves; they are inextricably linked, evolving from the same strong core.

Your Signature Work Checklist
To define the nature of your own Signature Work, think about the following:

- What are you most passionate about?
- What makes you come alive when you share it?
- The thought of sharing or delivering which idea or concept excites you the most?
- What would you want to share if you had no fear of criticism or judgement?
- Are there any topics that you feel endlessly curious, interested or fascinated about?
- Which subjects or ideas do you keep wanting to learn more about?
- What do you find endlessly inspiring?
- Which conversations and ideas do you most enjoy sharing?
- What scares you a little, besides lying close to your heart?
- Would you like to share any particular ideas or insights born out of your own struggles and challenges in your life?

Can We have the Love *and* the Money?
Most of us have been brought to believe we can either have the love or the money, but not both. For many of us, making our living doing the work we feel we were put on Earth to do feels like it's too good to be true. During the course of my work and travels, I have found most of us believe in a variant of these two ideas:

1. We have to make some sacrifices to earn a good living: we must go against our nature and do what is required

of us, usually by being compliant and doing what we are expected to do.

2. We can be outrageous and do what we love, follow our heart and express our gifts and strengths. But there is a price to pay – we are likely to struggle financially and to have to make massive sacrifices. We shouldn't expect to earn much as result.

Those were certainly the only two options I grew up believing were available to me, so they still resonate deeply with me. I followed both options: firstly, by selling my soul in my corporate career, and then by expressing my soul but not making such a good living in my own business. It took me a long time to get to where I was doing what I truly loved and allowing myself to be well paid for it. In short, like many of us, it has taken me a long time to value myself properly.

When asked whether he had a mission for himself when he became an artist, singer, songwriter and poet, Leonard Cohen responded by saying: 'I didn't want to work for pay, but I did want be paid for my work.' It's a beautiful distinction that serves all of us creatives well. I like to put it this way: *Do your work because you love it and are inspired by it – and when the opportunity is there, let yourself be well paid for doing what you are on Earth to do. But do it anyway!*

Creating an Authentic Brand around Your Signature Work

People who make a good living out of what they were born to do are often also very effective at creating a brand around their Signature Work. They realise that other people can't read their minds, nor is it their business to! It is our business to be clear about who we are, where our brilliance lies and how we can best serve our Signature Clients. They probably won't figure that out unless we tell them!

To get clear on your own branding, have a think about the following:

- Who are you for?
- What are you for?

- What will you and your Signature Clients achieve together when they do hire you?
- Can you prove your credibility through track record of helping people?

We could all do with branding, whatever level we operate on. We need to take to take personal responsibility for conveying our strengths and best qualities, what we stand for, our values and what we care about, and what we are capable of. This doesn't mean we have to become an obnoxious PR machine, but we do need realise that if we don't inform people, they may make their own assumptions, or there may just be a void where their clarity about us should be.

A couple of years ago I went to listen to soprano Renee Fleming talk about her life, work and the world of opera. She is active in helping to incubate future generations of opera singers and opera lovers. Now in her fifties and still at the top of her game, she said she found it amazing that new opera singers weren't not just taught singing skills at music college, but are also taught about branding, marketing and social media skills, in a way she never was. New singers are entering a completely different world from the one in which she started her career. They need to know themselves as singers, what they love, what they are brilliant at and what they would love to be hired for. They needed show up as their own authentic brand of singer.

The Power of Personal Branding

Now, I don't know about you, but I have very mixed feelings about the word 'branding'. It wasn't until 2012 that, to my own surprise, I started to fall in love with the idea. Until then, I had often judged branding as purely a commercial invention, all smoke and mirrors, although often very successful. Then, with a friend, I co-produced an audio summit about personal branding that thousands of people listened to. We interviewed fourteen leaders in their respective fields to ask them for their insights, experience and tips on creating an authentic and inspiring brand around what they did.

During my conversation with psychologist and author Robert Holden, I asked: 'Do you think we need another word for branding? It is a tainted idea?' And he gave me an answer that changed my life. He said: 'No, we don't need another name, but we do need another purpose of branding, other than purely commercial purposes.' Then it began to fall into place for me. I realised that personal branding could be a brilliant way to express fully our creativity, our spirituality and our values. We could take the influential things that brands do so well, and use them to elevate consciousness and make good people and their work have greater impact on the world.

What is the point of being brilliant and doing inspiring work if no one really understands you? Then we all lose.

The reality is that authentic and inspiring branding truly works. It means making a statement about the full creative expression of your purpose and who you are emotionally and intellectually. It can be about integrity, clarity, knowing yourself well and showing up with your specific gifts and capabilities, so you can make your contribution to the people you can uniquely serve.

Since then, I have run my own programmes on personal branding, leadership and creative branding and implemented them in my own business to great effect. But it is about conveying values, not just about making a noise. Personal branding can help good people show up in powerful and honest and impactful ways, turning potential confusion into impactful clarity:

- Personal branding is the ongoing illumination of the mystery of who we are.
- Inspired leadership branding accurately, clearly and powerfully expresses the reality of you, who you are and what you are capable of.

Simply put, personal branding stops people guessing.

Becoming More of Your own Brand

There are at least two ways of approaching branding:

1. Out of fear: *if I don't manufacture a unique brand around who I am and what I am doing, then I am probably doomed, so I had better do it properly and it well.*
2. Out of curiosity and even inspiration: *I want to understand myself, my gifts and my positive impact so I can convey the ways in which I can truly contribute and serve people.*

Typically, people say to me: *I know I am good at certain things, but I am not sure precisely what they are. I know people value what I do, but I don't really understand why. I know I have strengths but I can't see them clearly. There are some things I do some of the time, that, if I am honest, I would actually love to do more of the time.* To help them find their own answers, I explain that your true branding is:

- You at your best and in your authentic power.
- Your creative and leadership gifts fully expressed, successfully packaged and delivered to your clients.
- Your best work – your Signature Work or works.
- Loving what you do, and being inspired and inspiring, at some of the time.
- Making your greatest contribution.
- Being well rewarded for doing that.
- Potential clients are left in no doubt about what they should and could hire you for.

Branding at the Top

Sharon asked me to help her blossom into her leadership role, so she could create an office culture where people could do the best work of their career. She was the MD of a 500-person organisation, and her CEO had decided to step aside. She and the CEO had an agreement, whereby the CEO would advocate for Sharon at a global level so that

Sharon would then be regarded as her natural successor. But then the CEO didn't keep her side of the bargain.

Sharon was suddenly left to advocate for herself, a position that she didn't initially feel comfortable with. She held the belief that many of us do, maintaining that the quality of her work should be self-evident and speak for itself.

We spent one of our sessions diving into 'Brand Sharon', so that she could convey this concept clearly to the people who were deciding who the next CEO would be. And it worked. After our session, the board told her that until she had presented her pitch to them, they were going to turn down her application and look outside for a new recruit. Listening to her convey that level of clarity about who she was, what she has achieved and what she still had passion for and wanted to achieve, caused them to see her more clearly, reconsider and put her back in the frame.

I Never Knew that about You!

As part of my corporate coaching, I often encourage team members to share things about themselves with each other, and I've lost track of the times I've heard them say, 'Oh, I never knew that about you!' They then feel more connected to each other. Sharing more of ourselves and letting down our defences usually creates more empathy and emotional bonding.

As things stand, we are enough of a mystery to ourselves so are even more unknown to the people around us. We might forget that people can't see readily into our hearts and minds. Because we are so immersed in our own thoughts and feelings, we kind of assume that these must be obvious to other people too. But they aren't usually obvious, and people only know when we let them know.

Let Yourself be Known

Chris, a client, was concerned that people had put her in a box and saw her in a particular way, whereas she now wanted to be seen in a new way. She was known for one thing but wished to change this because she had grown and matured, and was evolving her brand.

As we talked, it became clear that she was younger, she might perhaps have embodied 'the arrogance of youth' to a degree – a reputation that had stuck with her in some areas of her professional community. But thirteen years later, she had matured into a successful practitioner, entrepreneur and an inspiring leader, and she now wanted to be a role model and encourage the next generation of young people. Instead of being seen as a dance practitioner and teacher, she wanted to become the inspiration that she had not experienced when she was younger.

She felt a little angry that she was not being seen that way yet, and I teased her by saying, 'They're not seeing you that way, because you're not showing up that way! You need to show up as you want to be seen.' What surfaced then were her fears that she might be judged all over again. She wanted someone to give her a 'big break' rather than have to commission herself and give herself the break. She felt that if someone else gave her the break she was looking for, this would somehow legitimise her new impulse, and she would have received a 'blessing' for it. So, we explored how she could let herself off the hook for any past mistakes, and how she could 'give herself that blessing,' and show up as how she now wanted to be seen.

Chris's example strikes me as typical. Once we have 'invented' our brand, we will probably have to keep on re-inventing it, which can be hard work. We might be tempted to look outside for further help and input.

But when we are following our soul's authentic path, while we are similarly likely to keep on evolving, we don't have to look outside ourselves so much as inside. We are more likely ask: *Who am I becoming more of now? What qualities are blossoming in me now? What creative and leadership gifts of mine are ripening? Who can I serve most effectively now?* And then we wonder how we can show up and express those new gifts. We don't have to start again from scratch; we evolve into the next chapter. There is a continuity here, rather than having to keep breaking off and remaking.

Personal Branding is Bespoke

Your brand isn't just a bunch of 'off the shelf' marketing strategies. It's about knowing why you care so much about what you are doing and what you are building, and letting your clients know why you're building what you're building. I think your people will love it when you share that with them. They will want to know about your heart as well as your head.

Start with how you got to this moment and how your journey to it has equipped you to help them. Tell your clients how you're going to help and why it matters that you do. Then show them how their lives will be better because of what you created. You may want to remind them what's at stake by acting and not acting. Your marketing doesn't have to be about promoting and pitching. Marketing can be a series of honest conversations between you and them.

Then you can begin to build a reputation around the results you help people achieve, which will help generate greater incoming interest in what you do.

Create a Niche around Your Branding and Signature Work

Your Signature Work can help you build a personal brand by creating your own authentic niche. You can create a niche around your Signature Work that is an inch wide and a mile deep. Because you love the area so much, you enjoy delving into it deeply to explore its different facets. Having a Signature Work, or even a series of works, gives you an umbrella under which to house all that you do. It can open doors for you to be completely free and expansive, able to go as deep as you want to within your topic.

Your Signature Work demonstrates and showcases your authority, thought leadership, self-leadership, experience and expertise. You get to tell stories about how you and your work have transformed people and situations, and then get incoming interest from people who want you to help them.

You Are Not for Everyone

A niche business accepts the idea that our service might be specialised and that our Signature Clients might number a select few – and that is perfectly OK. One of the most powerful things we can do for people is create a brand they respond to, heart and soul, thinking: *That's me, they get me! I have found a home for my mind/heart/soul. I am safe here. I have found someone I can trust.*

When I was running Inspired Entrepreneur, it was a niche business, but it was a pretty wide niche. Anyone running their own business was potentially interested in what we offered. Today, I see myself as a much more of a boutique business. I am no longer trying to please or serve everyone, or change the whole world, but I love to serve a few people 1:1 in much greater depth. I have found it a much more satisfying and actually much more financially rewarding way to work. In 2018, 90 per cent of my income resulted from coaching around twenty people. A bigger niche can appear to offer you greater security, but it won't necessarily. Many businesses fail precisely because they try to be too generic and appeal to everyone, rather than speak deeply to a few people, their tribe.

However, it takes courage to acknowledge and accept that we are not for everyone. It often feels like a bit of a dent to our ego, that can easily believe that everyone should like us, and that we could change the world if only everyone would listen to us!

Your Personal Branding Checklist

Marketing can be icky and appear to be all about selling stuff to people. Marketing done right is a true act of generosity. True branding is actually an act of service, helping you to find your Signature Clients to find you.

To define the nature of your own Signature Work, think about the following:

1. Who are you for? Who do you love working with? Who can you add most value to and serve most powerfully?
2. How are you positioning yourself in the market place? Top end, mid or low end?
3. What pain are your people in? What do they aspire to?
4. What is your Signature Work, your formula? Where are your people when you start to work with them? Where do you help them get to?
5. What are you at your best, playing to your strengths and experience?
6. Why do you love doing this work? Why do you care about it?
7. Why are you uniquely qualified and credible to be doing this work?
8. What is your joined-up business model? How many ways can people engage with you?
9. How do you get to be seen and known more widely? How do you love casting your net wider?

What Makes a Personal Brand Truly Powerful

Simply thinking Brand You is a great start, but many people spend thousands on branding and it still doesn't work commercially – it doesn't attract or serve the people it sets out to.

In my experience, there are three key elements to successful branding:

1. Your client is the heroine or hero of your brand – not you.
2. You position yourself as the credible guide to help your client triumph.
3. Your messages are clear and powerful and resonate with your Signature Client.

Many people spend a lot of time and energy talking about themselves rather than focusing on how to serve their clients successfully. They create a brand that talks about themselves, not about their ideal client. And the bottom line is that most people are not that interested in us individually. They are interested in how we can help them get out of pain, or how we can help them be happy or successful.

That said, you can demonstrate that you have travelled the territory that your clients are in; you have experienced their pain and you understand their aspirations. You have triumphed in some ways and your personal story should demonstrate that you are a capable guide who can help them achieve their own success. You know the terrain, the obstacles and the opportunities, and any short cuts that might make their own journey easier for them.

What Does 'Successful Enough' Look Like?

Many of my coaching clients find it helpful to consider what a 'successful enough' business would look like. How much income would that mean? How many of clients or customers would that represent? What is their brand and what form does their business take? Interesting, the process can also help them to relax. When we don't have a clear picture of what success looks like for us, it can easily seem like nothing we do will ever be enough. And that can trigger fear, whereas the process of envisaging it and quantifying aspects of it can move us from something potentially limitless to something that seems much more achievable.

This process is about shifting from a kind of scatter-gun approach to a laser-like focus, which helps us to concentrate on and attract the quantified number of people we can serve. You start to see yourself as more of lighthouse, shining your light, being a beacon for your ideal clients and then guiding them on their journey.

You have the power within you right now to triumph over your resistance, to show up clearly and powerfully in your work, leadership and life. But this needs to be accompanied by an understanding of how to release that power of yours. One of the most effective ways is through the power of devotion: through devotion to what you love, you will incrementally release more of your innate power. That is what we are going to explore in the next chapter.

CHAPTER 11
YOUR POWER OF DEVOTION

'People think I'm disciplined. It is not discipline. It is devotion. There is a great difference.'

Luciano Pavarotti, Opera Singer

I worked with Charles over several years. His world was completely alien to me; he was a stock trader, and had developed trading strategies that had yielded significant success at particular times during his career. Normally I would not have found working with someone in that area very inspiring, but what drew me to work with him was his character. He was dedicated to blossoming into his personal mastery, committed to leading himself as successfully as he could and exerting self-sovereignty. He wanted to be the best man he knew in his heart he could be, trusting that success would flow from there.

He had built up his credibility, to a point where he had been trusted with a fund of $200 million of other people's money to invest. The idea of having access to a fund of $200 to invest blew my mind! I could barely imagine the emotional dynamics and pressure at play in his life, the responsibility he had and how he managed his emotions.

We all seem to put obstacles in our own way, and most of us seem to put an upper limit on how good we'll let things get, or how successful we will let ourselves be. Early on in my relationship with Charles, I fed something back to him as diplomatically as I could. The conversation went a bit like this: 'You seem to have developed a way of analysing and picking stocks that, over two or three years, will bring a healthy yield. You have a high success rate. But in the longer term, you don't seem to trust yourself, your decisions and your own thinking. You keep giving in both to other people's fears and to your own. You make short-term decisions, usually based on anxiety, and then undermine your own system.' I was feeling brave so finished by saying, 'Basically, you screw things up for yourself!'

Luckily, Charles smiled, because it was clear he understood that was precisely what he was doing, and was grateful that his guilty secret was out. This was the growth in sovereignty he was seeking.

Charles worked with another analyst, who'd discovered that once Charles had made his decisions, he would have made millions for his fund if he had then left things alone for a two- or three-year period. The reality was that he often got freaked out by short-term fluctuations in the value of stocks, and either sold, losing money, or sold and made some money – but he would have made even more if he hadn't sold. He lost millions because of his fearful decision-making. He described to me how he would often go to the men's room and cry with fear when his stock fluctuated, and then come back and make decisions in that turbulent state.

I teased him, saying, 'If you just bought the stock, and left it alone for two or three years – even went on holiday and ignored the stock market – you would have done better than you've done now!'

It was his own interference that was costing him dearly. He was sabotaging himself.

We all have our own preferred means of self-sabotage – such as not following through, making excuses, causing arguments, alienating people, isolating ourselves, blowing things up, behaving arrogantly or undermining our own success. I think the underlying dynamics are often similar: we are afraid of our power, authority and sovereignty, and we don't believe we deserve to succeed. We resist letting things get really good.

Whilst it would have seemed more comfortable to conveniently blame the markets, his colleagues or the pressure of the job, Charles was able to start acknowledging that he was the author of his own problems. Only by seeing this could he begin to claim back his power. Both the problem and the solution lay in his hands. He acknowledged that he pretty much had a compulsion to act out of fear and adrenaline rather than 'being the captain of his own ship' and steering it through the short-term storms on the way to a safe harbour. He'd lost sight of his longer-term vision. Paradoxically, once we then made a decision about the way forward for him, the hardest thing for him was to do nothing!

I was reminded of something I had read in Timothy Gallwey's 'Inner Game' series of books. His premise was that we are all very capable and have enormous potential. That is a given. But what stops us is our 'interference' and for most of us our interference is fear, resistance, our inner critic, unhelpful beliefs and compulsions. His formula was: performance = potential, minus interference.

So Charles and I started working together on how, each day, he could reduce his interference so that he could realise more of the innate potential in him. He devoted himself to weaning himself off his compulsions.

I didn't see Charles again for three and half years, but when we did reconvene, he reported that his self-mastery had increased. His yields had gone from around 6 per cent to between 20 and 40 per cent, and he was now regarded as one of the stars of his industry. He had also started to unpack his own system so that he could share it with others. I was reminded of the wisdom of spiritual teacher Sadhguru, who said: 'For a committed person, there is no such thing as failure, just lessons to be learnt on the way.' Charles had discovered that his devotion to his area of expertise had opened new doors of mastery for him.

We often don't associate the word 'devotion' with business or with being entrepreneurial and inspired leadership. We tend to think of devotion as belonging to the realm of spiritual or religious practice, or the arts and the creative worlds. However, as the experience of Charles shows, devotion can be the key to unlocking business success, to self-mastering and inspired leadership.

Devotion Incrementally Dissolves Interference

A major reason why devotion is so powerful is because resistance hates focus and depth. Resistance wants to keep us shallow, distracted and unfocused – out of our true power; whereas daily devotion allows us to go deeper and stay focused, thereby dissolving resistance over time.

That's the path I think most of us are on when we are interested in our own growth and evolution. Through the process of ongoing devotion, we incrementally melt our own interference, and then the potential that has always been in us naturally comes to the surface. We regain our sovereignty and steer our ship more steadily, and are less prone to the short-term turbulence and dramas we may experience in life. But we may well need to pay close attention, as the changes are often small and incremental and easy not to notice.

At this point, our inner critic can also creep in and say things such as: *I should have understood this years ago. I've left it too late now!* You've probably heard the idea that the best time to plant a tree is twenty years ago, but the second-best time is now. Start new habits and devotions now. In the decades to come in your life, the new habits you begin today will yield dividends.

Devotion Means Acting in Anticipation of Inspiration

We can all have a powerful relationship with inspiration, but it won't necessarily just happen; we need to spend time actively cultivating our relationship with it. This means opening ourselves up to become receptive to the inspiration that is already there, even when we might think our inspiration and flow have deserted us.

As I mentioned earlier, I have sat down to write pretty much every morning for ten years now. Sometimes I don't always feel inspired, but by devoting myself to sitting down and writing anyway, the inspiration invariably begins to flow. I have written sixteen books so far. Have I written so many books because I am incredibly disciplined? No, certainly not. I am devoted to writing and developing ideas and then communicating them to serve others. I don't have to discipline myself to write – I love it, I am devoted to it. I now feel robbed if I don't get to write.

For the past four years or so, I have also published something on each of my social media channels every day. I partly do this to inspire people, but as much as anything I do it for myself, to be able to say, 'There, I have beaten my resistance again, today!' as I hit the 'Publish' button.

Inspiration does exist, but as we have seen, it needs to find you working. Rather than your sitting about, waiting for inspiration to strike, maybe the Muse is waiting for you to start work.

The Difference between Discipline and Devotion

The traditional view is that in order to succeed, we need to develop great discipline. Often discipline is something we think we need to impose on ourselves, as we might become lazy and unfocused if left to our own devices. However, I have seen in the case of myself and clients that when we try to impose something on ourselves, there usually comes a time when we either rebel or give up.

In contrast, devotion helps us enter a kind of spiritual slipstream and to attract good things to us. With devotion, you are not using force on yourself; you are drawn forwards by love – by what you love doing and by what truly inspires you. Devotion is about taking care of your inspiration and creativity, not demanding it take care of you. Devotion is a combination of head and heart.

I have shared this idea around the world for over a decade now and it is often met with something akin to a shock of insight and recognition. It's as if we think the only way to really succeed is to be incredibly disciplined and most of us don't feel we have the necessary discipline, or that we even want to be that focused and disciplined. Maybe it's part of the Protestant Work Ethic (which we looked at in Chapter 2) that many of us are familiar with: the belief that we have to drive ourselves to make ourselves succeed.

The way I see it, this is the core difference between discipline and devotion:

- Discipline is needed to get yourself to do something you would actually rather not be doing.
- Devotion enables you to do what you naturally are inspired to do or be.

Of course, sometimes you may need to use some discipline initially to get through your resistance and reach your flow of devotion. And there are of course some things we know we need to do for our wellbeing that we may never grow to love – such as exercise and doing tax returns.

I am obviously waving a flag for there being significant aspects of our lives where inspiration and devotion act as guiding forces. It comes down to whatever creative and/or spiritual expression you are drawn to.

When I reconnected with Liz Trubridge on the *Downton Abbey* set back in 2013, I asked her in a lull between takes if she was still enjoying leading the cast and crew, as this was her forth series. Her response was: 'It is a privilege to do this. Yes, I still love it!' But there was something about the energy with which she said *privilege* that I found inspiring. No, she wasn't jaded, she wasn't bored. This was an expression of her devotion and she loved doing it. Each day, each season and each scene was inspiring to her.

Devotion Builds Inner Strength and Spiritual Musculature

In Chapter 5, I shared Gary's story. He wanted to start a business to support men. But although he wanted to get his ideas out into the world, he hadn't really written very much. I sensed there was a current of inspiration and creativity in him and that he had messages he was here to share. He was inspired to write but wasn't yet clear about what he had to say. His voice, his river of creativity and content, was deeply buried within him. He couldn't access it easily, because it had been buried for such a long time.

I got Gary to do some writing and share it with me. I then invited him to commit to an ongoing, daily writing practice. We kept in touch. A little further down the line, he told me that instead of waiting for 'huge swathes of time' that he could devote especially to writing, he was now going to write within the realities of his life, as we had discussed; these included his everyday commitments to his family, paying the mortgage, personal growth and development, and travel for work.

As he devoted himself to writing and expressing himself, Gary reported: 'I can "go there" a lot more easily and quickly now. It feels more like an ongoing dialogue rather than an occasional visit to my creativity.' The river of creativity and ideas were much closer to the surface for him now, and consequently much more accessible. Within a few months of his devotion to writing, not only was he beginning to believe that he had something valuable to say, he was keen to look at how to package this message in products and services, and start earning his living from them.

I had gently challenged Gary not to wait for the huge tranche of time that he had dreamed he might have one day, but instead to create a more regular devotion to his creativity through shorter visits. This had worked for him, and made it easier for him to access his creative flow even when time was limited, whether on his commute or at home. Regular conscious contact with our inspiration, creativity and leadership will bring these forces closer to the surface and make them more readily accessible for us. It's not what we do occasionally that makes the biggest difference to our creativity and leadership, but what we devote ourselves to consistently.

What Are You Devoted To?

In my experience, the best leaders are devoted to at least two things:

1. Something bigger than themselves, such as a universal idea that they are individually taking a stand for in

this world. They want to embody peace, compassion, inspiration, hope, nurturing or a number of these qualities. Many want to be the best woman or man they know in their heart they can be, and to be most loving or inspiring presence they can be in any moment.

2. Their own personal and spiritual growth and evolution. As we saw in Chapter 7, I am of the opinion that self-acceptance contains much greater power than self-improvement. Many of the best leaders I know are devoted to being more at peace with themselves, as well as their continual personal growth and expansion.

Devoted to Several Loves – Maybe You are a Renaissance Soul?

Many of us don't have a 'single love', but several. During our first session, Veronica and I went through her many interests and activities. After half an hour, it was clear there were at least three areas that she was devoted to:

- labyrinths and the idea of pilgrimage generally;
- a lifelong love of the harp;
- writing – to share her insights, passions and reflections of life and spirituality now that she was sixty.

One way you might be limiting your creative expression is by limiting the canvases on which you express yourself. Think of Leonardo da Vinci – inventor, sculpture, inventor, architect, scientist, engineer, mathematician, geologist, writer, cartographer and botanist. Imagine if someone had taken him to one side to have a word in his ear: 'This is all very well, Leonardo, but when you are you going to get focused and do one thing really well? When are you going to get a proper job?' He and the world would have been much poorer if Leonardo had taken that kind of thinking to heart.

Some of us love to dive deeply into one or two areas, whereas others love to explore many areas. There is no right or wrong way to be creative. To me, the important thing to know the shape of your own soul and live in alignment with it, rather than live out of the programming and conditioning you were brought up with, which might have urged you to 'get a proper job'.

Devotion and Worldly Success

In May 2018, I was fortunate to spend a day with author Elizabeth Gilbert. She explained that when she was young she'd made a pact with life to commit to writing, because in her heart she felt that was what she was put on Earth to do. To her, writing became almost an act of prayer. Yet, although she devoted herself to the practice, most of her early work barely caused a blip. Then, in 2006, she published *Eat Pray Love*, which suddenly took off and sold twelve million copies, and was turned into a Hollywood film starring Julia Roberts.

Liz has carried on writing since that success simply because she loves the very act of writing and not just the material rewards that it may or may not bring. Writing offers her an intrinsic joy. She is also clear that while she is aware she might have already published the most commercially successful book she will ever write, she knows she will keep writing for the rest of her life.

The Power of Perseverance

Devotion is also about recognising that we are likely to trash our own work at some point and feel like it's game over. The challenge then is to persevere even when it feels like there is no hope left.

In *The Hero's Journey*, Joseph Campbell describes the archetypal point in stories when all hope appears to be lost. Every great story has at least one moment when the hero thinks their dream is over, the odds stacked against them are too great, and they feel defeated.

I don't know how many of these moments I've had – dozens, maybe hundreds. But here's the funny thing – I am still here! The chances are that you have experienced these moments too, when there feels like there's little point in carrying on. Then something happens, a mentor or friend says something, we have a flash of insight, an opportunity arises, we start to see things differently, and suddenly our vistas open up again. *Game back on!*

Weathering Emotional Turbulence

Bestselling author Philip Pullman writes wonderfully about the experience of writing, and his devotion to coping with the emotional ups and downs.

> **'How to Write a Book' by Philip Pullman**
>
> First, make a plan. Get a large piece of paper, the largest piece you can find, and some of those little yellow Post-It Notes. Write down an idea for a scene on each of the yellow stickers and stick it somewhere on the paper. When you have a whole bunch of them, say about forty or fifty, move them around till they are in the best order you can find. That's the plot.
>
> Next, you make up some characters. You need a mixture of good ones and bad ones, old ones and young ones, rich ones and poor ones, pretty ones and ugly ones, and so on. That way every reader will have someone to identify with.
>
> Then you need to do some research. You want to write about life in a medieval castle? Go to the library and look it up. You want to know what kind of clothes they wear in the north of Finland? Go and find a National Geographic. You need to do lots of research. Make photocopies of everything you need. The more research you do, the more interesting your book will be.
>
> Then... Well, then you take your big piece of paper with the plot on its yellow Post-It Notes, and your careful notes about the characters, and your photocopied information about castles and Finland, and you bundle it all up into a heap and you throw it all away. Forget it. It's useless. And you start writing something completely different, something that you have no knowledge of,

> something that just came into your head, something that is utterly strange to you.
>
> And you're seized by a fever of excitement. It's like falling in love; it's like setting out on a thrilling voyage; it's like no other joy in the world. You are possessed. You feel radiant. You give off light. But... There comes a time, part-way through (in my case it usually happens around page 70), when you fall out of love with it. In fact, you begin to hate it. You read it over and you are convinced that never has anyone, in the history of the world, written anything so slack and feeble. You are ashamed. You can hardly look at yourself in the mirror.
>
> But because it's too late now to do anything else, and because you're a stubborn so-and-so, you write on grimly until you get to the end. Then you put it away and decide to be a football player or a film star or a brain surgeon instead. Anything must be easier than writing. But after a little while you think... No, it wasn't that bad. And... When I started it, I was really excited.
>
> And... Maybe if I looked at it again, I could tinker with it and cut that bit out and maybe bring that character in a little earlier, and it might work. And you get it out and think... Hey, this is actually not bad at all. And so you cut it, and you fiddle with it, and you change the order of this bit and that bit, until the story works. If it were a table, it would stand up without falling over, and you could put things on it and they wouldn't slide off, and from some angles it might actually look quite pretty...
>
> Then you do it all again. Get a large piece of paper.
>
> Well, that's all I know about writing books. I've been doing it for over thirty years, and I shall do it till I die.

I find it very reassuring that we are all standing on the same ground; this experience isn't personal, but universal. When we are doing what we are put on Earth to do, and we are devoted to it, we are still likely to hit 'all hope is lost' moments.

Navigating the Bumps in the Road

Devotion means keeping on going even when we hit bumps in the road. When you get a smooth ride, enjoy it and make the most of it. If you hit a bump in the road, don't worry. There is always hope, even when you can't see it yet. Although it may feel like a catastrophe, it rarely is. It's just a storm cloud. Know that this too shall pass.

We often make permanent decisions based on temporary feelings. Most temporary discomfort passes, sometimes quickly, sometimes in time. To me, that is about developing our real pro side: as professionals, we know we are devoted and in it for the long haul, and we will not be thrown too far off course by temporary turbulence; and even if we are, we will find our way back in to the saddle.

This is the path of mastery.

Devotion is the Path of Nurturing Self-Awareness

'We're all nothing without the Muse. But the pro has learned that the goddess prizes labour and dedication beyond any theatrical seeking of her favours. The professional does not wait for inspiration; he acts in advance of it. He knows that when the Muse sees his butt in the chair, she will deliver.'

Steven Pressfield, ***Turning Pro***

American business magnate Warren Buffet has great technique for developing self-awareness. He books a meeting with himself at the end of every day, during which he goes for a walk and thinks about how he has reacted or responded to issues during that day. Where he finds that his thinking has caused him stress, he identifies any underlying beliefs, behaviours and habits that he wants to change. He says, 'The chains of habit are too light to be felt until they are too heavy to be broken, and we then function in our dysfunction.'

I have been lucky to attend several recordings of the UK BBC Radio 4 hit comedy series *Just a Minute,* hosted by the brilliant Nicholas Parsons for fifty years! I also went along to another event in London where he talked about his life and work. He shared that even at the age of ninety-four, he still listens back to the show to see what he did well and what he could improve.

Committing to the Process

I have been a writer now for many years. But it probably took me about a decade to take my writing seriously. As I mentioned earlier, I used to write just when I felt like it, when I had nothing else in my diary, or when I had a deadline to meet. However, for the last ten years, I have committed myself to writing for two hours each morning in a local café, including at weekends. As long as I'm not ill or anything urgent is going on, I go out to write.

Do I always feel inspired to write? No! But usually within a few moments of sitting down at my laptop, I find myself accessing a flow, the inspiration arrives, and the ideas, words or projects takes shape. In that area of my life at least, I have developed an 'inner musculature', a strength of devotion rather than a discipline. Yet if a coaching client asks me to speak to me at 9am, I still find myself feeling slightly embarrassed to say: 'I am available after 11am because I write and work on my creative projects from 9 to 11am every day.' My inner critic still chimes in to say, 'Who are you to think your writing is so important that you put yourself first?' But it is an appointment with myself that I am not going to break, no matter what the outcome of a particular writing session.

There is something about acting consistently rather than occasionally that has enormous power to it. I watched a fascinating documentary about the band Coldplay in which lead singer Chris Martin was talking about the art of song writing. He said, 'No one really knows where songs come from, or whether any more will come. All our biggest songs take ten minutes. But you only ever get them by spending hours and hours and hours with the other ones, and then one suddenly comes through. And you just receive it. Then the band develops the song. My hit ratio is about one in ten.' He is devoted to the practice of song writing, knowing that

90 per cent of his songs will be abandoned and rejected, but he presses on with it in order to be available to the 10 per cent that arrive seemingly out of nowhere, as a result of his devotion. Your best results in the long run are always made up of what you are willing to do in the short term.

Staying the Course

Through devotion, you will gradually become the captain of your own ship. From experience, you know that there will be beautiful days, there will be days when you are becalmed, and days when you doubt your own ability and whether you have what it takes to steer the ship to your chosen destination. There will even be times when you encounter storms and curse yourself for ever having left the safety of the port.

But when you finally arrive at your destination, much of the journey will be forgotten. You got there – and that's all that matters. You have stories to tell, people to inspire, eyes to widen. You will inspire others to go on their own voyages and discover new territories. You are a person of wisdom, no longer imprisoned by your fears.

The Terra Firma of Consistency

Consistency is a facet of devotion. With respect to inspired leadership, it means being consistent with our statements, consistent in the content we create, consistent in the way we chip away at the problem we're seeking to solve. Consistency is usually very generous. And the best thing is that we only have to make the choice to be consistent once. After that, it's simply a matter of keeping our promise.

Leadership is about consistency and generating more inspiration in the world; it means choosing to show up and make our contribution. In the final chapter, we are going to dive into the power of your unique style of leadership.

CHAPTER 12
YOUR POWER TO OFFER INSPIRED LEADERSHIP

'If your leadership isn't about drawing the best out of yourself and others, what the heck is it about?'
Liz Trubridge, Executive Producer of *Downton Abbey*

The call to leadership often arises out of a combination of frustration and inspiration. In Chapter 8, we met Shilpa, who founded her new school and who then went on to found another. She is now planning her largest school yet, a potential global flagship. But the reason that she started out in the first place was to create a school near to where she lived in India that she would be happy to send her daughter to. Shilpa has a great love of the Goddess and wanted to send her daughter to a school where her daughter's soul would be kept intact rather than squashed or be processed through the 'education sausage machine'. Shilpa felt that an inner call of inspiration that she needed to respond to.

That is one of the things I find most inspiring: supporting people to get past their own fear and resistance and successfully answer their own call to offer leadership in this world. It is, for me, one of the most courageous and inspiring things we can do with our lives. When we are offering the world something it might not be asking for yet, that it might not even realise it needs, but which is born out of our own heart and inspiration, that is the ultimate inspired leadership.

Inspiration is the Eternal Animator

Inspiration is what animates artists, entrepreneurs and great leaders across the planet and throughout history. Something inside us wants to be expressed and shared with the world, and despite all the odds and all the resistance, we have to keep going, chapter after chapter. It is the ultimate act of personal sovereignty.

Leadership isn't just a position, it's a choice – and it is a choice that is available to you in each moment. I think every act of love, inspiration, creativity or forgiveness is an act of leadership, and while it might take courage at times, we can make those decisions in any moment.

New Inspired Ways of Leading, Please!

On New Year's Eve 2016, I listened to a radio documentary called 'The Future of Leadership'. It was presented by author and leadership expert Margaret Heffernan and in it she interviewed leaders from a variety of organisations, including Apple, Microsoft and the armed forces. She asked them what leadership might look like in the future. Red-cape leadership, with the idea of the leader as 'saviour', was now over, she argued. Inspired leadership, she said, is not about concentrated power, but distributed power. In this model of leadership, power is no longer concentrated at the centre, as great leaders genuinely seek to empower others. Inspired leadership means partnership, not dominance – which can become tyranny. It is about cooperation, mentoring and support. Leaders are no longer thought gods and, indeed, they are called to account like never before. Leadership is now about learning to enable the creativity and entrepreneurial capacities of everyone.

I found the whole programme fascinating, and as Margaret completed the show, she reflected on metaphors of leadership. She cited war and sport as being two common ways of approaching it. But her favourite metaphor for leadership was this: 'Leader as gardener, the one who does nothing but help to create the conditions in which everyone and everything can flourish.' That's it, I thought, bullseye! I love leaders who consciously seek to create the conditions that enable people to do their best work, contribute their best qualities, and fulfil their potential. Starting with themselves!

The Inspired Leader as a Loving Gardener

The wise gardener knows they don't really have power over *what* they garden, but they do have power *with* it. The gardener knows that they can't really force, reward or manipulate the best out of plants (or people). The gardener doesn't yell at the seeds to grow or threaten to sack the seedlings if they don't develop into saplings at the right pace. The gardener knows the potential that exists and then supports and encourages to help the seed – or person – fulfil that potential. Great gardeners know rhythms and have patience, and understand seasons. By providing the necessary nutrients and protecting their charges from harmful toxins, gardeners know they have a good chance of success.

Like great gardeners with their plants, great leaders are incredibly skilful at working with their people, cultivating and nurturing and nourishing them. They never stop learning because they love discovering how to become even more effective in what they do. They are connoisseurs of talent; they love, appreciate and nurture talent, both their own and those of others.

Leadership is the Desire to Generate More Inspiration in this World

Being found inspiring, and being told so, can often be a pivotal moment in our lives. One of my clients e-mailed me recently to arrange our next session, and said: 'After a session with one of my students, they told me that they found me inspiring! I have been called many things in my life, but never inspiring!'

To me, Will was obviously doing his job successfully. I believe that the primary job we have in leadership is to inspire and, more precisely, to be the cause of more inspiration existing in the world. I think everyone has the capacity to be inspiring. I believe there is a well-spring of inspiration in you, waiting for you to mine it and show up with it in your own unique ways.

However, if you want to be the cause of inspiration, then you have to keep your own fires of inspiration alight. I think it's pretty hard to be truly inspiring if your own sense of inspiration is dim. So another of the primary jobs in leadership is to *keep yourself inspired.*

I am fully aware that 'keeping myself inspired' doesn't appear on most people's to-do list, especially those who are busy delivering their leadership to the world. Yet one of the conversations I most love having with clients is around the subject of: 'How are you going to keep your soul aloft? How do you and are you going to feed your own sense of inspiration?' It is a simple but immensely powerful discussion to have, and something that I'd encourage you to think about too.

The 'Why' of Leadership

So much about leadership is focused on the 'what' and the 'how' of leadership, the techniques and strategies – and these are all important. Yet I think we need to be asking other important questions, such as: what is the purpose of your leadership? Why do you want to lead either yourself or others?

Four really important questions to ask yourself are:

1. What is the purpose of my leadership?
2. What am I aiming to achieve?
3. Who is my leadership for?
4. What does my leadership look like?

From Command-and-Control Leadership to Enabling Leadership – from Fear to Love

In a sense, this whole book is about one of the most powerful and significant shifts we are all being called to make. I would describe it as an evolution of thinking, even an evolution of consciousness. I have touched on it before in this book, and it is easy to describe – from fear to love. Yet it is not always easy to embody.

Although much of the history of the human condition has been about control and domination, I don't think we are here today to control or dominate each other, but to free ourselves. I think we are here to be part of an evolution in the ways in which we relate to each other, to help enable each other to fulfil our innate potential.

Increasingly people don't respect authority for the sake of authority. So many sources of authority have become tarnished. We now only willingly follow people. We follow those who inspire us, whose worldview we engage and resonate with. Essentially, today you have to be inspiring to your people, or they simply won't follow you. You can no longer demand compliance.

Yet while it's simple enough to say that this approach is what is called for now, and we might be tempted to judge others for being stuck in 'old' ways of thinking, the rubber hits the road when we actually bring this shift into our own moment-by-moment activities.

Why Judgement Doesn't Usually Solve Problems

Traditional styles of leadership are often steeped in judgement: this is right/this is wrong; this is good/this is bad; we are good/you are bad. The ego loves judgement, and we can spend a lifetime refining our capacity for it. Yet judgement can actually reinforce a problem rather than solve it, by dragging us further down into it. Judgement of ourselves makes us feel bad, and judgement of others can lead to disagreements, conflicts, fights, power struggles and impasses. As a friend of mine says, judgement is like shooting fish in a barrel: you can't miss! So much to judge, so little time to do it. In many respects, judgement is easy. But it doesn't really uplift us or solve the problems we face.

It is time to spend less energy fighting what we don't want, and more energy creating what we do want. A core difference between old styles of leadership and new leadership styles is that the latter are much more focused on acceptance rather than judgement. Instead of concentrating on what we believe is wrong with people, we seek out what is right with them. Instead of trying to invalidate them and pull them down, we try to lift them up and inspire them.

I always loved the idea put forward by the visionary architect Buckminster Fuller, that the best way to replace a current paradigm is to create something so inspiring and exciting that the old way of doing things will naturally die away. So I would suggest that we spend less time criticising old ways of leading and concentrate instead on offering our own inspiring leadership that people will naturally gravitate to.

There is a saying that 'values unite while beliefs divide'. I believe we need leadership that unites us around our shared values rather than operating through divisive beliefs. What if we genuinely explored leadership as a means to create more peace, kindness, compassion, understanding, openness, creativity, love and kinship?

Changing the Thought System with Which We Offer Leadership

Inspirational leadership is less about dominant personalities and more about thought systems. Each of us embodies a mash-up of thought systems based on fear and control, as well as those based on love and inspiration. When we are run by fear, we tend to be judgemental and to act in a similar ways; likewise, when we are fuelled by love, acceptance, a desire for transformation and inspiration, we tend to act in fairly predictable ways. Essentially, as we have seen, there are only two forces at work: those of love and fear. And because we all embody elements of both, our leadership journey is likely to take a similar trajectory – away from fear and returning to love. It is the journey I think we are all on in life.

I went to a seminar in London in March 2016 about 'Leadership and the Enneagram', where one of the presenters, Russ Hudson, suggested: 'We live in a dysfunctional system. It's hard to be functional when we don't have many functional leadership role models to aspire to.' We certainly do live in a system that is many ways dysfunctional, but it doesn't need to stay that way.

The Significance of an Inspiring Worldview

As we saw through the example of Desmond Tutu in Chapter 7, inspired leadership is about having a vision, a worldview, a story, a lens and narrative through which we see the world and make sense of it, and through which we help others see the world and make sense of it too. Powerful leaders provide clear information and direction, and are often great storytellers. They inspire people to consider possibilities. They speak to deep universal truths and tell inspiring stories about who we are and why we are here.

Sadly, over and again, many people in leadership roles play to our anxieties instead, through a narrative of fear: *If you don't vote for me, or get behind me, or do as I say, then terrible things are likely to happen to you. If you don't buy this, you are going to feel bad about yourself. You are either for me or against me!* We are all familiar with those kinds of messages.

Yet there is also a deep hunger for a style of leadership that tells more inspiring stories. Stories that speak to the goodness of people, their potential for love, creativity and transformation; that explain we are one human family and we need to care for each other; that we are all precious and bring unique gifts and talents to the party.

One of the reasons so many people are drawn to the world of personal growth and the human potential is because of the appeal of these sorts of narratives. It is wonderful to be told you have so much potential in you, that you can grow; that you are not a victim and can change from feeling powerless to being powerful. We love to hear the stories of people from not-so-promising beginnings who have gone on to achieve amazing things and become better people. While there can be a fair degree of naiveté sometimes around what is really involved in achieving our potential, there is no doubt that personal change and transformation are possible for us all.

Offering the Leadership You didn't Experience

Over the years, I have found that many of us are inspired to offer a style of leadership that we often didn't see modelled when we were younger. Indeed, our lives might have completely lacked what we seek to stand for in this world. This is really courageous stuff. Many of us might have felt wounded by the leadership of others, abused and victimised by people in positions of power and kept in our place rather than encouraged to bloom. This might even have happened in our own family, or in the wider world. And yet we feel the call to offer a different kind of leadership to ourselves and others. There is something in us that knows things don't need to be this way.

We too can be the pioneering leaders.

We have taken on wounds, gone into the dark, suffered and gradually learned to heal, forgive and transform. We have felt bad about ourselves and triumphed by feeling truly better about ourselves. We have gone deep into our own darkness and found the light again. We have been able to find the love in us that wasn't always modelled for us. When we can heal enough of our own wounds, we find the love and inspiration in us that has been in there all along, but lain dormant.

I suspect there is often a strong connection between leadership and parenting. I suspect we are often looking for the parents we didn't have to meet our unmet needs, until we learn to be our own powerful parents and meet our own needs effectively.

Surrendering to Something Greater

When I first went into therapy, I didn't feel like I had grown up in circumstances that would set me up for a happy life: a depressed and often suicidal mother, a sister who always seemed to find fault with me, and an emotionally absent father. I grew up with massive self-doubt; I felt like a real victim, and I also invested a lot of energy in seeing myself as a victim.

Part of me believed: 'I chose this! This is my training ground!' And then another part of me thought: 'What on earth was I thinking? What a stupid thing to have done. I am not ambitious, I am stupid! This is too high a mountain for me to climb. I can't do this.'

One day, I hosted Marianne Williamson at an event where she spoke about *A Course in Miracles*. She explained that the *Course* is not really about self-help, the point being that you can't really help yourself, because it was your thinking that got you where you are in the first place. However, you can be helped by a higher and more inspired way of thinking. While our ego might have us believe that we are doomed and without hope, the *Course* teaches that there is a power that wants to lift all of us up to our 'rightful' place. As we saw in Chapter 5, it is our thinking that leads us into various cul-de-sacs and difficulties. And it is our surrender to this higher power that lifts us back up again.

Inspired Leaders Allow Great Things to Happen

What if we truly believed that great performances simply wanted to happen? When I was helping Liz Trubridge, the *Downton Abbey* producer, consider her style of leadership, she shared her belief: 'Magic and miracles actually want to happen for us in each moment. We have to open to them and allow them. This allowing, rather than resisting or trying to control, is a very feminine quality – and equally available to men as women. I seek to create the conditions that allow the magic and miracles to happen that I believe naturally want to occur. And it is wonderful when we succeed as a team to allow that magic to come through.'

Great leadership operates from the presupposition that people want to shine and want to give their best. So many of us are caught up in our own self-judgement that we don't allow ourselves to blossom. Inspired leadership can reach into our hearts to help us believe in ourselves. Great leaders, then, are often great enablers. They are secure enough in themselves to allow other people to be and to give of their best. They don't try to hold people back, control them or keep them in their place. They allow the great things to happen that want to happen. They believe:

- Inspiration wants to happen.
- Creativity wants to happen.
- Great performances want to happen.
- Great work wants to happen.
- Peace wants to happen.
- Collaboration and partnership want to happen.
- Healing wants to happen.

Secure Leadership

I have met many leaders who have been prone to a feeling that most of us experience: insecurity. They harbour the fear that they can be replaced, that there might be someone better for the job than them. They can feel a little fraudulent. This can all show up as in excessive controlling behaviour and wanting to keep people in their place.

So one of the questions I invite people to think about is: 'How you can be so good at leadership that people will want to support you and be on your team, rather than replace you?' (As I write this, we are in a full flow of Brexit negotiations in the UK. Slightly mischievously, I have often wondered, 'Why isn't the EU and its leadership so inspiring that people wouldn't dream of wanting to leave it?')

Two Things Most of Us Have to Deal with as We Step into Our Leadership

A few years ago, I was having a conversation with one of my friends and mentors, Jeff Allen, about the joys and challenges of offering leadership, and what true leadership means. He suggested that the two dynamics you are likely to face as you step in to more of your leadership are:

1. Envy: people being envious of you, your success, happiness and achievements.
2. Criticism and judgement: others finding fault with you and trying to bring you down.

Which doesn't make leadership sound very exciting, does it? And that is why I think devotion is such an important concept, because if we stay true to our own path, we can gradually understand that people who are envious or critical are really in fear and pain, which is why they act like they do.

I'd like to turn again to *A Course in Miracles*, which been a great teacher to me in so many ways. As will be clear by now, one of its most significant teachings for me has been to understand that there are only ever two things going on – love and fear, and that what isn't love is a call for love. Inspiring leadership understands this. When you have done enough inner work, you begin to understand that those people who appear to attack you are actually in great pain. In a distorted kind of way, they are asking for your love, and they hope you have some kind of gift for them.

Blossoming into Leadership

I have seen enough of leadership to know that no leader I have ever met is the fully formed article. They all have gifts and they have problems. They have things they find easy, and things they really struggle with. But something inside them makes them keep going and keeping growing.

For you to blossom into your fully realised leadership, what nutrients might you need?

Once we have responded to inspiration's invitation to self-leadership, and to draw the best out of ourselves, many of us feel a call to offer leadership to others. This isn't usually because we occupy a position of power, far from it. There is simply something in us that wants to help, that wants to serve. We have managed to reduce our own suffering and become happier, creative and more powerful, so we want to offer what we have learned to others too.

I can't make anyone listen to me. What I can do is share ideas and experiences that create a resonance with people. This is why I am willing to share my personal experiences openly, and as a result I find I often connect with the personal experiences of others. It's satisfying to see myself mirrored back in other people's experiences and to know other people see themselves mirrored back in mine. I think sharing our experiences makes us feel less alone, and realise that we are all part of one human family.

The Power of Responsibility

Obviously, one of the key elements of leadership is our willingness to be responsible and to take responsibility. Responsibility is such a loaded word, though. When some of us hear the word, we automatically think, 'OK, so I'll be the one you can blame when things go wrong. I'll martyr myself!' In other situations, we see people accept positions of leadership and then look for someone to blame for their problems, as we saw in Chapter 9. They seek scapegoats.

Yet most of us don't find blaming others massively inspiring. What do we find inspiring is people's honesty, and their willingness to take responsibility for their actions. We tend to find genuine emotion inspiring. When people take, rather than deny, responsibility, and apologise for their shortcomings when necessary, we usually find it easier to let go of our grievances and hurt against them, and even understand and forgive them.

Carrying Responsibility Lightly

Many leaders seem to believe that by showing their seriousness, they prove what good leaders they are. They might, for example, talk about working night and day to show how much they care. They talk about the personal sacrifices they make. We tend to think of responsibility as being heavy, and about being burdened by our responsibilities. Yet while it's true that responsibility can feel heavy, it is possible to carry our burdens and responsibilities with a sense of lightness.

I told one MD I coached how inspiring I found her, because she carried her responsibilities lightly: she led a company with a £60 million turnover and nearly 500 employees, yet I always sensed her genuine enjoyment of her leadership and how she kept her energy as high as she could, so that she was a living example for her employees of someone who took their work seriously but who had fun doing it. She was happy to lead and to lead willingly.

Responsiveness as a Leadership Quality

You may have heard the idea that responsibility is the ability to respond. One of the most important aspects of inspired leadership is responsiveness. The deeper we dive in to ourselves, into our own gifts, creativity and sense of inspiration, as well as our own challenges and suffering, the more clearly we start to see things and to respond to them appropriately. While we are not responsible for each other's emotions and experiences, we can be responsive to these.

I learned a lot about responsiveness from the journey I have been on with my mum and her dementia since she went into a care home in October 2013. Her dementia has gradually got worse over the years. For the first few years, she had her own telephone line in her room, so my sister and I could call her and she could call us.

Then, one day in December 2015, my sister and I received around eighty-five calls in a single day from Mum, demanding that we take her out of the care home and bring her home. I managed the first fifty calls reasonably well, but after that, I found them so difficult I wanted to cry. I didn't know what to do. I had Power of Attorney and was in charge of Mum's finances and wellbeing. When she was still of sound mind, she had said clearly that she wanted to live out her final days at the home, but now she demanding I take her out. I felt understandably conflicted. Was I forcing her to stay somewhere she didn't want to be? Was I doing the wrong thing? Should I just 'hold her' and stand firm whilst she went through her journey? What else could I do? In the end, that was the course of action I decided upon, although I felt guilty, cruel and so sad about it.

When I visited Mum a couple of days later, she had no memory of making all the calls, and was in a relatively good mood for her. That did my head in even more! My sadness began to turn into anger. I could see that the care home was doing a pretty good job for Mum and the other residents, but couldn't they see how difficult a journey this was for us relatives too? We were suffering as well. Why didn't they try to do a bit more for us? They seemed oblivious to our suffering – to my suffering.

I had e-mailed the activities manager of the care home, Irma, and asked if I could speak with her, so we sat down together and she listened while I poured my heart out. Although part of me wanted to rage and blast the home for not seeming to care about us relatives, I ended up crying and Irma listened kindly and compassionately.

Then she helped me understand more of Mum's internal world. Irma explained that, in effect, I had lost Mum already. The woman I had known as my Mum had largely gone. I was now dealing with a different person. Because of the dementia, Mum no longer responded so well to reasoning. What she really wanted was to feel loved, accepted and validated. She wanted to hear that she could have what she was asking for.

I took Irma's words on board. The next time Mum said to me, 'I want to go home', instead of trying to reason with her and explain why we couldn't do that immediately, I said, 'Sure, I can take you home. Let's have a cup of tea and cake, then let's see about that.' She seemed to respond well to this, and of course her dementia was so bad that she would soon forget her request, or that I had agreed to it. She would often then revisit the question, but with no memory of our previous conversations.

I had already started to speak with friends who were on their own journeys with parents suffering from dementia, and realised that most of us hadn't realised that as the dementia progressed, we needed to learn to respond to our relative's needs in a whole new way.

Of course, responsiveness is a two-way street. When I was in pain after my mum's phone calls, Irma at the care home was responsive to me. It meant the world to me that she didn't just dismiss me, but sat and listened to me while

I was in pain. I was beginning to glimpse how I could turn the pain I was experiencing into some kind of gift, both for myself and others. Irma had led the way and walked in to meet me in my place of pain when many people would have walked out. Now we were both offering a form of leadership and guidance to others.

Transforming Pain into a Gift

As we learn to solve a problem and deal with our own difficulties, there arises in many of us a desire to help others. We feel the urge to ease the suffering of others if we can, because we know that suffering ourselves. Inspired leadership is often born out of personal challenges and problems, as we begin to transform them. In some areas of leadership, our difficulties may qualify us and gives us authority.

You lead because you are the living proof of triumph – what have you triumphed over? What do you still struggle with? Where can you offer hope?

Not Rescuing, but Accompanying

Inspired leadership is not about rescuing other people but accompanying them on their journey.

Alison had a background in mental health, and was now the CEO of her own care company. She was preparing the business to sell on so she could move full-time into coaching and public speaking. As she developed her coaching practice, it began to dawn on her that back in her old mental-health days, she felt a great pressure to provide all the answers for her clients. She used to feel that she was there to help fix them, and that her success was correlated to how well she did this. Effectively, she thought she had to rescue them.

She was now beginning to see that her power didn't lay in her ability to rescue her clients, and she didn't need to have all the answers; in fact, she didn't have all the answers. Her skill lay in her ability to help people discover their resourcefulness for themselves. Some people might still come to her, wanting to be rescued – but she didn't have to try to do it. She could filter them out. She wanted to coach people who were willing to take responsibility for their own growth.

She was well aware of the drama that can occur when people won't be fixed – and how easy it is to become invested in their change to our own detriment. She realised that truly inspired leadership means believing in people's innate resourcefulness and becoming skilful at drawing that out to help them discover it for themselves.

Inspired Thought Leadership

While many of us don't want to create an organisation, we do want to offer our inspiration and our knowledge, strategies and hope, based on our experience. I think of this as wanting to offer inspired thought leadership. Thought leadership means becoming a guiding light in your area, able to lead people skilfully across the territory that you have successfully navigated.

As inspired leaders, we become guides. Once we have led ourselves somewhere meaningful in our own lives, we will have gained an understanding of a particular emotional terrain. We then feel the call to help others, to share what we have learned and come to understand. We want to share the wisdom gleaned from our experience. To me, that's a definition of love and generosity: sharing our wisdom to make life better for others, and exercising power with compassion.

Every day, we witness so much abuse of power. This can lead us to shun power and see it as a bad thing, and to judge those in leadership positions. Yet power, when used with integrity and compassion, can act as a force for the good of the whole, not just the few. So don't be afraid of your power; simply use it as a force for good.

Leaders as Awakeners

'The biggest barrier that human beings face in touching, experiencing, and knowing the Divine is unwillingness to transcend logic.'

Sadhguru

When we show up with the light we bring and act upon our inspiration, we serve as awakeners for each other in ways that we may largely be unaware of. In a sense, we are 'obliged' to be inspired – there are people out there who are waiting for us to show up and lead the way.

We are so interconnected. My friend Catherine used to be a recruitment consultant in the 1980s, with big shoulder pads and addictions to match. One evening, she went to see Cirque du Soleil at the Royal Albert Hall in London. As she watched the performance on stage, she suddenly remembered that she had wanted to be a clown as a child. She sat and cried at the memory of the dream buried in her heart. This led her onto a journey of recovery and to train to become a sacred clown, then to travelling the world, both clowning and teaching clowning.

Because we are so interconnected, you have no idea of the impact that your showing up in your inspiration might have. Each of us who is awakened and who shows up in our inspiration acts to awaken the soul of others.

Please give us your inspired leadership; we need you and the light you bring.

POSTSCRIPT: PLEASE DARE BOLDLY

The following excerpt comes from President Theodore Roosevelt's speech 'Citizenship in a Republic', which he delivered at the Sorbonne in Paris on 23 April 1910, and it encapsulates much of what I have been saying in this book:

It is not the critic who counts; not the man who points out how the strong man stumbles, or where the doer of deeds could have done them better. The credit belongs to the man who is actually in the arena, whose face is marred by dust and sweat and blood; who strives valiantly; who errs, who comes short again and again, because there is no effort without error and shortcoming; but who does actually strive to do the deeds; who knows great enthusiasms, the great devotions; who spends himself in a worthy cause; who at the best knows in the end the triumph of high achievement, and who at the worst, if he fails, at least fails while daring greatly, so that his place shall never be with those cold and timid souls who neither know victory nor defeat.

Leadership is an imperfect art. No one knows everything about it, it is easy to criticise and generally much harder to embody. Yet what an incredible adventure is waiting for those who accept the invitation of inspiration and embark on that journey.

Useful Addresses

I live in Finchley, North London, and I teach and coach inspirational leaders around the world, in person and online. I also give key-note talks on inspirational leadership at conferences and in organisations.

If you would think I could contribute to you or your team, please do get in touch and we can arrange to have a conversation. If I think I can help, I will make a formal proposal to you.

My website is: **www.iamnickwilliams.com**

You can contact me on: **nick@iamnickwilliams.com**

You can connect with me at:

www.linkedin.com/in/iamnickwilliams

www.facebook.com/nickwilliamsauthor
Instagram: **iamnickwilliams100**
Twitter: **@nickwilliams1**

Read peer praise here:
iamnickwilliams.com/about/peer-feedback

Learn more about my speaking experience here:
iamnickwilliams.com/signature-work/keynote-speaking

Find out more about my media experience here:
iamnickwilliams.com/about/media

Discover a list of my other books here:
iamnickwilliams.com/books-2

Inspired Leadership Coaching and Mentoring
If you see yourself as a pioneer or visionary, I would love to help you realise your full leadership potential and support you as you move into your next chapter. Please contact me to arrange a conversation.

ACKNOWLEDGEMENTS

To **Helen Bee,** for our 23-year journey, the growth we continue to experience together and the fun we have had – and for being happy that I go out to write every morning.

To **Sushi**, our cat, who literally walked in through our back door and into our lives in August 2017 and who has brought us so much joy. He is like the child we never had.

Continuing thanks to **Dr Chuck Spezzano** for opening my mind twenty-five years ago to new ideas of what leadership could be.

Thanks also to **Jeff Allen** for friendship, healing and our conversations on leadership.

Thank you, **Liz Trubridge** for your friendship and sharing your experience so generously with me. Our conversations have been pivotal and life-changing for me, opening my heart and mind. You have been so important to me.

Deep gratitude to **Archbishop Emeritus Desmond Tutu.** My evening in your company was truly life-changing, and to all the people I met through *The Rainmaker Foundation.*

Thanks to **Steven Pressfield** for continuing to be an inspiring influence on my thinking about resistance and its impact on our expression of creativity and leadership.

Deep thanks to all the clients that it has been my privilege to work with and to be inspired by.

Art Giser, for the amazing energy work you teach.

Enormous thanks to **Liz Galbraith** for our years of energy work together. This weird shit really works!

Nikki Richardson, for your natural leadership, and for being a champion and an inspiration to me.

To **Cat Knott,** for friendship, laughter and insightful support.

Adrian Bourne, for our regular meetings at The Institute of Directors, for laughter and friendship as we get older and hopefully wiser.

Luisa Di Lallo, for friendship, wonderful cooking and your willingness and courage to start over.

Peter Carey, for pool, friendship and being an inspiration.

Irma Aleshe, for all you do to bring joy and understanding to the residents, staff and families at my mum's care home, and the laughs we manage to have when I visit.

And continuing thanks to the mind behind *A Course in Miracles,* and the ongoing inspiration to keep healing fear and returning to love

Thanks, finally, to the **Elders** in *The ManKind Project* circles to which I belong – you are 'my tribe'.